Growing
ORCHIDS
THE
SPECIALIST
ORCHID GROWER

Growing
ORCHIDS

THE
SPECIALIST
ORCHID GROWER

J. N. RENTOUL

Lothian Publishing Company
MELBOURNE · SYDNEY · AUCKLAND

A Lothian Book
Lothian Publishing Company Pty Ltd
11 Munro St, Port Melbourne, Victoria 3207

First published 1987
© J. N. Rentoul 1987
Reprinted 1989

National Library of Australia
Cataloguing in Publication Data:

Rentoul, J. N. (James Noel), 1909–
  Growing orchids. The specialist.

  Includes index.
  ISBN 0 85091 279 2.
  ISBN 0 85091 280 6 (pbk.).

  1. Orchid culture. 2. Orchids. I. Title.

635.9'3415

Typeset in Garamond by Solo Typesetting, South Australia
Printed in Singapore

CONTENTS

INTRODUCTION

As this book was being produced in 1986 we were within the approximate time of the bicentenary of orchid growing as a pastime. The date when it commenced is not completely verifiable, but it was apparently between 1770 and 1800 in Britain and Europe.

The logical approach to the present is naturally through the history of the cult, and the literature of the period when the centenary was proposed in 1900 is voluminous and very beautiful.

In 1901, in Volume 7 of the *Orchid Review*, published as the authoritative monthly journal of British orchid growers, the editor, R. A. Rolfe, contributed an article celebrating one hundred years of orchid growing. Rolfe reviewed much of what had happened in those hundred years and according to this account 'the year 1800 seems to have witnessed the advent of the first East Indian orchids, when thanks to the exertions of Sir Joseph Banks three species of Geodorum and *Acampe multiflora* were introduced, together with *Aerides odoratum* from Cochin China.' It was also the year in which Olaf Swartz named the Australian *Dendrobium linguiforme*, probably the first or certainly among the first of the new genus which he created in 1799.

Naturally all the orchids of those early years were species collected from the forested and verdant areas of the total known world. Horticulturists and garden lovers were excited by the stories which travellers brought home with their plants, and very soon those first plants from Cochin China found themselves bundled into unsuitable conditions with other species from the Americas and other zones in a hopeless miscellany which was destined for certain extinction. The destruction continued until about 1835, when the methods of growing the plants were totally changed. Veitch's *Manual of Orchidaceous Plants* records something of the folly, in the remark about the plants which poured into the country that they were 'too often only to tantalize the purchasers with a transitory sight of their beautiful flowers and curious forms and then to languish and die.'

Information and advice from people like Alan Cunningham from Australia, Skinner from Central America, and Gibson from north-eastern India, the collectors Lobb, Motley and others from the Indo-Asian and Javanese areas put an end to the destruction. This knowledge probably was first interpreted and put into practice by Joseph Cooper, a gardener in one of the larger private establishments in England. He reduced the temperature of the growing conditions and opened the ventilators. The change was remarkable, and William Hooker is recorded as having said in 1835 of Cooper's work: 'I must confess that the sight of this collection, whether the vigorous growth and beauty of the foliage or the number of splendid species blossoming at one time be considered, far exceeded my warmest anticipations.'

The owners of these large collections of orchids and exotic plants were the first specialists. They took the credit, but the reality is that Cooper, Paxton and others like them were the innovators. Perhaps the necessary information filtered down to them as instructions, but they were the growers as distinct from the owners.

The owners increased their collections by buying stock from various importers, buying at auction or by direct purchases from nurserymen like Veitch, Low, William Bull and others. Some of the owners also sent their personal representatives to various parts of the world to seek 'novelties', gather them and bring them back to Britain and Europe to enrich their collections. Although America did not have many such owners at that time they did enter the cult at a later period.

Once the demand was created the trade increased and provided occupation for a number of recognised collectors. These men covered great distances, often in unexplored and untravelled places, to find the goods to supply the demand, as outlined in *Growing Orchids, Books One, Two, Three* and *Four*. Apparently there were no female collectors, but there were several very competent growers in Britain and elsewhere.

Some idea of the size of such collected plants is available in the early volumes of the *Orchid Review* and other contemporary literature. One example is typical of plants stripped from the habitats in the first hundred years of the cult, namely *Laelia albida* (Bateman and Lindley), not an easy species to cultivate. Exhibited by Joseph Chamberlain and produced by Smith, his grower, in the year 1899, it carried 32 spikes with an aggregate of 139 flowers.

It is impossible to imagine as we approach the bicentenary that such plants still exist in the habitat. It is also impossible to visualise private collections of species orchids in the numbers and magnitude of that of Joseph Chamberlain, the plan of whose glasshouses appears on the next page. The industrial revolution in Britain and Europe created the wealth with which Chamberlain and his counterparts bought the plants so cheaply and squandered them so freely.

In *Growing Orchids, Book Four*, on the Australasian orchid families, I suggested that only 2 per cent of the original number of the Australasian orchids remained. I see no reason to doubt or amend that figure and perhaps even that was an optimistic assessment. In view of the over-collection and destruction of the natural orchids of planet Earth, that figure may realistically be considered as one which is relevant world-wide.

The species of all genera are again in the 1980 decade claiming attention from growers. Although the habitats cannot be reafforested and regenerated into ecological zones where our almost lost species could again populate them—at least in the short term—every effort should be made to propagate the orchids and retain what remains.

Orchids are unlike other plants. As a total family they come from the floor or surface of the earth, some even subterranean; from the tops of the trees and all the zones in between; from the depths of valleys and the tops of mountains. But it is possible that such information is seldom taken into account in filling out our desires.

The standard of cultivation of orchids should be raised, and one way of doing this is to acquaint all growers, and particularly beginners in the cult, with the nature of the plants they wish to grow. This book is written to that end. It cannot be everything to everybody, but it may prevent the mismatching of plants and conditions which plagued the cult from its beginnings and in some ways persists into our bicentenary years.

The reference books listed in the back of this book form part of the author's private library and the taxonomy in general is taken from it. But as it is almost impossible to keep up with this phase of orchid growing some of the references may be wrong. As noted in *Growing Orchids, Book Four*, these books are written for orchid growers, not taxonomists, and they may also not please botanists as such.

A great amount of work goes into producing books such as this series: first one must grow most of the genera involved and then go from reference to reference, researching as far as possible all the stages in nomenclature through which an orchid may be taken; after photographing some 3000 subjects a selection must be made

An indication of the scope of the pastime in Britain in the 1880s can be gauged from this plan for a range of glasshouses and ancillary buildings erected for Joseph Chamberlain. The central unit or division number 10 measured 24 feet by 32 feet (7·3 metres by 9·7 metres). The size of other sections can be worked out from that figure.

This period was near the centenary of the pastime and could be termed the golden age of the cult because so much wealth was devoted to it and it preceded the thoughtless plundering of the world's orchid species.

The various numbers of the sections represented: 1, the entrance to the range from the house; 2, the conservatory;

3, the boiler house, which no doubt also served the domestic requirements from the two large boilers housed in it; 4, the fernery; 5, the stove or tropical section; 6, East Indian orchids; 7, cattleyas; 8, calanthes and phalaenopsis; 9, the display house; 10 to 14, miscellaneous plants; 15 and 16, orchids; 17, primulas; 18, odontoglossums; 19, the poultry shed; 20, glazed corridor connecting all the houses.

It was an east–west structure, span-roofed and built in brick. In it were housed at times as many as 2000 to 3000 odontoglossums, 1000 plants of *Laelia anceps* and many other species represented in double and triple figures.

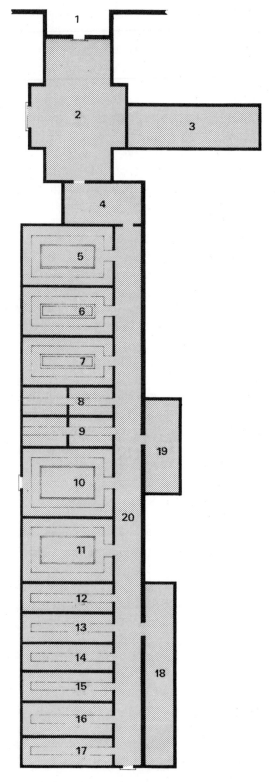

and finally all the information must be put together in the hope that the finished book may equal the amount of thought that went into it. Books are an art form like so many other human activities and however painstaking and tedious the work of authors, inadequate critics can tear them apart very quickly. But authors are at least entitled to presume that those critics would be able to do the job as well if not better.

The nomenclature throughout this book does not conform to the code for reasons which should be obvious to most readers. The generic titles have been italicised only where specifically used, with species names appearing in italic face throughout. No apologies are made for this format, which is simple and understandable for the people who will be the majority of its readers.

1 THE SPECIALIST

One may well ask if it is necessary to be a specialist in order to grow orchids. The simple answer is no, if it is understood from the beginning that orchids are no different from any other plants and flowers which grow on this beautifully endowed planet we call Earth.

A specialist is never satisfied and it takes only a few minutes looking through any orchid journal to note that there are numerous people cross-pollinating flowers of various genera in a wonderful orgy of miscegenation while looking for that miracle flower which no-one has succeeded in producing and everyone will want.

The specialist does not wait for that miracle flower—he wants the best available at the moment and will spare no effort to make it flower to its greatest potential. To show that there is even-handedness about the whole thing, the 'he' could as easily be a 'she'.

The specialist's aim is to assemble a representative collection of any genus as a central point; about this is gathered perhaps a rather miscellaneous group of fill-in material with similar tolerance to whatever conditions prevail. But the main genus remains paramount.

The specialist will realise when a collection is becoming unmanageable and will preferably have decided on its size when planning it. A cymbidium specialist would acquire the best range of colour without being unduly influenced by the somewhat spurious standards occasionally applied as the prerequisite for judging the genus.

The specialist in any other genus would need to work out a plan of operation which may be based on the very things which would be avoided in cymbidiums, particularly if the genus is cattleya or phalaenopsis, for example. There would be times in either instance where small could be as beautiful as large and size was not a qualification for inclusion.

Most of the information required by the specialist is in the literature of the cult, some of it very old, some quite new. Some is very difficult to trace but worth all the effort. Some is very expensive, but again worth the price. Every step along the road must be planned and it will be found that in some instances the oldest practices are the best. In all, specialising is the most wonderful part of orchid growing. It could well be asked if it is worth all the trouble. It all depends on what 'makes one tick', as a colloquialism has it.

It is not necessary to have a lot of money in order to establish a specialist collection, but if the beginning is to be modest it will take longer. From a small start, the major part of a collection can be slowly replaced over a period, but remember that it cannot be continually remodelled. One must be content to let a lot of innovations in colour or number of flowers to the raceme slip by without regret.

Determining how many plants can be accommodated in the space available is the first step. Working on the principle that the space between them should equal the space each plant occupies offers a sensible approach, considering the purpose in view. If we continue with cymbidiums as our example, assuming that every adult plant will eventually be grown in a 250 millimetre pot (about 10 inches), a single row of ten would occupy 5 metres or just over 16 feet.

Although it may be difficult to set a fixed size for the collection when the project is launched, it may be a good idea to set a limit of fifty plants, as even this number of top quality cymbidiums will be hard enough to assemble. The bench space necessary for the fifty at maturity and full production would be 5 metres by 2½ metres (about 16 feet by 8 feet). If possible it should be an island bench, so that every plant is totally in view and accessible all the time. This aim will determine the design of the enclosure necessary to house the collection. It can be done in other ways, and this is of course the concern of every individual who takes on such a task.

There is no need to suppose that other orchids cannot be grown with cymbidiums, but preferably they should not be suspended over them. The needs of the principal genus must be considered before those of the fill-ins which are necessary to round out any orchid collection.

Selecting the plants would be the hardest task. Probably the best criterion would be colour. Shopping around when buying any orchids is worthwhile. It does not matter how old a clone may be, if it has the right colour and other qualities keep it in mind and buy what is available. If one has to buy mericlones to get a particular cymbidium it is better to buy two than one. Every plant has a different growing rate. It will be appreciated, from what has been said so far, that building a specialist collection is a long-term project and one requiring patience and determination.

As the plants are growing, however long they take, at the first opportunity a propagation of each should be taken out and grown on a separate bench. This should be a continuous process, so that there is an adult flowering plant on the specialist bench every year. It will be obvious that in reality this has perhaps more than doubled the space necessary, but this is the only way in which to manage a specialist collection of any genus. Do not crowd that specialist bench with one more plant than indicated, and do not allow one plant to rob another of light or air.

The experience of building up such a collection of orchids offers the best enjoyment that could ever be gained from the pastime and quite a few facts about the lives of cymbidium plants will emerge. One of the first of these is that no clone gives the same sort of flowers in consecutive years. Whether this is true of the original species has never been the subject of investigation so far as I know. But over the years a series of photographs of the same clone and often the same plant have shown fairly wide divergences in colour, size and shape. Some of this may be attributable to human errors in our cultural habits, but that is part of the pastime.

Another thing which becomes obvious is that the best plants are those brought on from small propagations, starting with perhaps leafless back-bulbs and working upward to flowering size. On average, the best size for reproduction of the peak result in most cymbidiums seems to be from five fully leafed pseudo-bulbs.

There is no necessity to limit the size of the project in cymbidiums; each grower must determine how much space and how much money can be devoted to it. The principal thing is to stick at it until it becomes worthwhile. It is possible to have a wonderful collection of cymbidiums numbering only 20 clones and allow time to dictate at what point any of these are eliminated and replaced. But once a decision has been taken, be sure that all of the clone is culled out and replaced.

A final point should be made. Some cymbidiums flower on new growths each year, but others never flower on new growths, only on pseudo-bulbs made in the previous year. Do not expect any of them to change—if they do so it will be a chance flowering and not regular. Note down which category every plant falls into, so that in projecting annual results each one should indicate by January whether it will flower or not. Any clone which must grow a pot full of pseudo-bulbs should not be considered. There is too much time wasted, however good it may be.

If miniature or novelty cymbidiums are to be part of your specialist collection, they will need to be chosen with as much care as standard size plants. Analysed as a separate section in hybrid form, if the same harsh standards for miniatures were enforced in forming a collection it is fairly safe to say that only about 5 per cent of the plants now being cultivated at this bicentenary period in orchid growing would be kept in cultivation. The ratio of miniature cymbidiums to standard specimens in the collection would have to be fixed and kept at that level. Allow for the fact that in general the miniatures must be elevated to the same level as the standard plants and in many instances suspended in hangers to allow the flower racemes to develop. They should not be hung over other cymbidiums.

In general all the recommendations on the formation of a specialist cymbidium collection are applicable to any other genus which takes the fancy of a grower. Some of the information and recommendations are enlarged on in the chapter on cymbidiums.

So far it has been assumed that this cymbidium grower has asked himself or herself the question 'In what climate do I live?' It is the question which must be asked in every instance of the desire to become a specialist in any genus because it has direct bearing on success. The climate of a region should dictate the choice of a main genus.

Other genera may have different habits, but the essential factor in establishing a collection is again the space allotted to each plant. What are referred to as cattleyas in this book could be far removed from that genus by as many as four infusions of interbreeding with other genera. These are principally rhyncolaelia, laelia and sophronitis. They do not radically change the general character of the flowers, but they do alter the actual size and nature of the plants. This may have to be taken into account in setting limits for a collection of cattleyas planned along similar lines to cymbidiums. Once the limit is reached, the cut-off should be firm. If it becomes necessary to cull, the whole clone would be culled and not just a piece which may occupy either a first or secondary role as a representative.

As made plain in another chapter it is possible to build a cattleya collection of monstrous size and still not exhaust either the colour or quality factors. However, another influence on the collection is the non-ageing of many of the genus even in species form. This is something not really affecting a cymbidium collection, which appears to be an ongoing production line with no apparent limits in the 1980 decade.

The formation and housing of a cattleya collection is not very different from any other genus, but the space factor is less constricting than for cymbidiums. The plants may be almost in contact, pot to pot, provided light and air co-ordinates are sufficient. The restriction would be only on ability of the grower to handle the number, keep the plants free from pests and individualise them more than cymbidiums because of their seasonal flowering.

It could be asked with some justification if one would be able to form a specialist collection of any genus without importing from other countries. The short answer is yes. Although a variation could occur from one country to another in, say, cymbidiums, there would not be so much variation in shape or size of the flowers.

Unless money is no object and time must be considered it may take five or more years to collect and flower twenty-five first-class cymbidiums and at least another five to complete the fifty cited as a satisfactory number. In that ten years there are sure to be changes in the general pattern of new flowers, but the temptation to start again should be resisted and the best possible job done with the clones already in hand. The time to cull is after the project is complete. It is very easy to be sidetracked by the glossy and appealing advertising of suppliers, but remember that any plants imported must go through quarantine and it could be anything up to three years from their release before their best flowers are produced.

This outlook would prevail for most genera, but the specialist making a collection of compatible species orchids may need to take much longer to fill out the collection to his satisfaction. (Again the 'him' could as easily be a 'her'. There seems to be no difference between them in the matter of orchids.)

For the ultra-specialist who wants an individual collection of plants not available to anyone else, there is only one route to follow. Almost the total group of plants must emanate from seedlings and no propagations of those clones would be parted with. It is a hard-headed business proposition, which could be applied to a part of a collection. It has been done, and perhaps the reputation of such growers is usually expressed in terms which could be out of place in this book.

The ultra-specialist must also remember that his or her seedling stock must not be accommodated at the expense of the main group. As at least ten of a cross-pollination should be bought, sufficient space must be set aside for them. Within reason any genus can be accommodated in temperate climates and *it takes only the right ancillary equipment to change some of them to sub-tropical or tropical.*

2 ORCHIDS AND CLIMATES

The basis on which all orchid growing rests is the division of species and hybrids into three categories: those which will grow in cool climates; those which prefer intermediate climates; and the last which must have almost tropical conditions throughout the year to survive and flower. Of course that is a gross over-simplification, and we must do better than that and begin talking about arrangements for conditions which are developed to counter-act natural climates.

The over-simplification also fails to take into account the blurred outlines which divide the three categories. In reality they scarcely exist.

The natural climate in which you live should influence the choice of the orchids you should cultivate. You must understand its variations and annual cycles and what is needed to meet its challenges. Human nature never follows the easiest of paths and most growers wish they had some other climate than that which is theirs.

Those who wish to excel in a genus or a collection must make some commitment which does not challenge too deeply the environment in which they propose cultivating the plants. All orchid growing is artificial once any sort of enclosure is used to overcome the restrictions imposed by the natural environment; if any growers finish up in mediocrity it is usually because they failed to face up to their initial problems.

In this chapter ways of meeting these challenges will be considered. After all there is little scope for changing the climate outside the enclosures, and all the advantages possible must be taken of the resources available inside the glasshouse or whatever else is the growing base.

MICRO-CLIMATES

There are subtle differences in the climates inside any enclosure, and these should be understood and used. Enclosure should be taken to mean any area which can be isolated by closing doors or ventilators. Where shade-cloth is used for walls very little can be isolated.

If an enclosure has a maximum interior height of 2½ metres (about 8 feet) there are several micro-climates between the floor and about 2 metres (about 6½ feet). From there to the apex there is virtually no change.

Internal climates are governed by external climates up to a point. Thus in temperate regions with maximums of about 30 degrees Celsius (about 80 degrees Fahrenheit) and perhaps odd days above that, the summer interior uncontrolled temperature could be as high as 40 degrees Celsius (over 100 degrees Fahrenheit) and more. With winter minimums of 5 to 10 degrees Celsius (about 40 to 50 degrees Fahrenheit) the uncontrolled interior temperature would be approximately the same as outside. This could be qualified by interior humidity, but only slightly so. These figures give a rough guide to understanding extremes of climate on the interior of an enclosure.

The positioning of such an enclosure, particularly a glasshouse, has a definite effect on interior climate. The position and aspect should decide the type of orchids which are grown in it, a subject comprising the major part of this book. Probably the greatest effect of position is on the micro-climates of such a glasshouse, to which we return.

If a thermometer is suspended in an enclosure midway between the floor and roof it will register about the average temperature between the air at floor level and about the roof area. Thermometers should be among the first pieces of equipment bought, one a straight-out measuring device and the other with movable mercury followers which may be released after a reading is taken.

The floor zone is naturally the coolest of the micro-climates of the enclosure, and good use of the zone should be allowed for in design and construction of the benches. The floor zone will not accommodate many plants if the benches are of normal height. However, if you choose to grow a genus originating in a naturally cool zone—for instance, pleione or masdevallia—then benches should be set low to suit, taking advantage of the micro-climate with the lowest summer temperatures. These could be artificially restrained to that level in a temperate climate ranging as high as the figures given above.

MICRO-CLIMATES

The floor level offers the lowest temperature of any enclosure. This can be intensified by correct watering and the use of an evaporative cooler.

For greater effect, the air stream from the cooler may be directed over a separate container of water, although most models contain water.

In this situation the orchids which need a moist, cool climate will grow to perfection. A genus in this category is sarcochilus and there are many others which need similar special growing techniques.

Other micro-climates are to be found at bench level. This picture shows a 'wet-bench' which provides suitable conditions for moisture-loving genera such as odontoglossums. The bench has a solid top and contains within its edging a bed of durable solid material, like gravel, which retains moisture for an extended period. This bed may also be topped, like that illustrated, with a layer of growing sphagnum moss. If the environment is correct this moss will grow during the warmer months of the year to such an extent that it will provide another layer of insulation and coolness. When this is combined with correct air flow through an evaporative cooler it is possible to lower the temperature at plant level to a considerable degree.

Where only a few plants are intended to be grown in that cool zone they may be suspended simply from the normal bench.

Bench design as well as bench height give some control in using the next micro-climate. In general benches should be a little lower than hip height so that access to plants is not made too difficult. The climate of such a bench is intermediate for an open bench and a little cooler on a closed bench covered with a layer of moisture-holding material like scoria or small gravelly stones or moss. The difference in temperature between the floor and these benches could be as much as 3 to 4 degrees Celsius (about 6 to 8 degrees Fahrenheit) and the difference between an open mesh bench and a closed moist bench about half those temperatures.

At least three micro-climates have already been noted in this one enclosure. At least one more zone can be utilised by suspending a group of plants midway between the benches and the roof. They should preferably be epiphytes. This three-tier regime is usually forced on growers by space problems rather than need for micro-climates. However, the four exist and the plants should be chosen to occupy any of them more by experiment than in other ways. It is only by using these micro-climates that most growers are able to cram so many diverse orchids into their houses.

Another micro-climate can be provided at bench level by creating adequate air flow. It is suitable for epiphytic orchids, which in their native habitats receive occasional drenchings which quickly drain away, leaving the root systems dry until the next application of water. A mesh bench such as this, together with appropriate potting material with good drainage, allows fresh air to flow about the plants all the time. This is the guiding principle behind cultivation of all epiphytic orchids. At the same time, the air flow must not be too dry, otherwise it fails to duplicate the natural sequence of events to which they have evolved over a long period. The open mesh allows moist air to rise from under the bench to create this atmosphere, and everything should be planned to ensure this.

A fourth micro-climate is to be found above the benches and against the walls of glasshouses. Preferably do not hang plants from the roof itself, whatever the structure. Provide for suspended plants by erecting separate pipe frames, or fix sheets of light mesh wire to the end walls. Keep the load off the roof members. In this micro-climate the warmest environment in the structure may be found, with the plants protected in winter by rising warm air.

Plants which are growing well in any of the micro-climates should not be moved to another simply for convenience. They should be left where they grow best. Appreciation of the available micro-climates and the suiting of orchids to each is a first important step in the pastime.

There is quite a lot beyond ordinary controlled glasshouses and reference to climates. The subject varies from cultivation in interior enclosures in living rooms, and extensive collections may be grown quite happily in cellars—uncommon features of Australian house construction but quite common in cold countries. These systems are well covered in other books, but none of these odd systems offer scope for creating such micro-climates and need careful attention to detail such as selection of plants.

Window-sill cultivation or growing orchids in sunrooms is not for the specialist: there will be small reward and poor plant life. My record in orthodox cultivation is more than fifty years for a couple of plants, which would have been impossible for indoor or window-sill cultivation. Weigh all these factors carefully and consider the circumstances in which the plants are to grow. None will last for long in human living space.

In climates with extremes of cold or heat, such as regions where sub-zero temperatures may occur for some weeks in winter, followed by extremes of heat in summer—and there are many such areas in the orchid-growing world—some genera may be cultivated success-fully and others may never give satisfaction. The tropics impose similar restrictions, and micro-climates are most difficult to devise and operate. An example of this could be trying to cultivate cymbidiums in the tropics; it is not an impossibility, but quite difficult.

It must be obvious from all the foregoing that micro-climates are integral parts of the habitats of all orchid plants growing naturally. These vary even more infinitely than any we can devise. In the tropics plants on or near ground level grow in a warm, humid and mostly still atmosphere; the epiphytes in the middle stage of forest growth have moderate air flow; while the plants in the open or on exposed tree tops have a constant and rapid air flow about them. The plants in that lower micro-climate seldom or never suffer

CLIMATE CONTROL
The unit in the top illustration is designed for internal use in a glasshouse to maintain minimum temperatures. If used internally a thermostat controls both the fan and the heater and the operation becomes intermittent. If the two functions are separated as in the unit illustrated, the fan operates continuously as an air circulator using outside air and an internal thermostat controls the heating function, warming the fresh air as it is introduced. The lower illustration shows the 90-millimetre ducting which distributes the air. It is bored with a 5-centimetre circular cutter at suitable intervals, and the plastic pipe can be turned to blow the air in any direction.

dehydrated root systems, while those in the middle and upper levels are subject to regular saturation and dehydration. This will be understood by most successful growers, although they rarely consciously analyse the factors of plant survival; but the unsuccessful will never appreciate or may entirely miss this simple fact of orchid growing. Achieving the basics may be difficult but not impossible targets in extreme climates. Growers in temperate climates could be envied because their modifications toward either cooler or warmer climates are comparatively easy to install and maintain.

In zones with radical extremes where summer temperatures may reach 35 to 40 degrees Celsius (about 100 degrees Fahrenheit) and in winter may fall to below freezing point, for most orchids the lower temperature range is more decisive. Providing warmth for warmth-loving plants is neither inexpensive nor easy. Some will survive short periods of cold but none will survive at freezing level. In providing for that type of climate, basic design should start with the enclosure itself. It would need to be fully enclosed, such as a glasshouse; preferably double-glazed or at least with an inner lining of plastic film in the roof and most of the walls if they are glazed. Double-glazing is described in *Growing Orchids, Book One: Cymbidiums and Slippers*. Depending on the genera grown, cooling in summer may be as necessary as heating in winter. This can be provided by means of a single unit. Although the initial expense of two independent systems may be a little high, they would carry out the functions a lot better.

This example shows how a difficult natural climate can be modified to a comfortable interior that may induce orchids to grow and flower. The high summer temperatures must be reduced by at least 5 to 10 degrees Celsius (about 10 to 15 degrees Fahrenheit), and the winter extremes brought up to a minimum of 12 to 15 degrees Celsius (about 50 to 55 degrees Fahrenheit). It is most unlikely that heating and cooling units will reach this efficiency, but the aim is to control as far as possible the outer limits.

The micro-climates of such temperature-controlled structures in radical external climates would not be as definite as in temperate zones, but they would still be there in moderation and capable of being exploited to assist various genera to produce the results asked for.

Moderately cold climates are no different from radical climates in the need for artificial conditioning of enclosures, but there is less need to worry about the upper limits on more than a few occasions in the annual cycle of the plants. Those days are probably within the tolerance range of most orchids if a little common sense is shown by growers.

Dissipation of unnecessary warmth through evaporation of moisture is a common phenomenon—humanity survives solely because of it. For plants also it is climate control at the basic level, particularly in conditions which would otherwise be disastrous for artificially cultivated orchids. The so-called odontoglossums are an instance of an otherwise climate-controlled genus being successfully grown in enclosures.

Control of humidity is relatively inexpensive. A meter will fairly accurately register the level and is necessary if control is manual. Automated controls are inexpensive for adjusting ventilation and humidifying the atmosphere or lowering its moisture content and this was illustrated in *Growing Orchids, Book One*. Automatic ventilator controls must be carefully serviced because they are affected by humidity and may fail to carry out their function.

Turning to interior house or window-sill cultivation, each attempt at this sort of cultivation is beyond advice because no two rooms are alike. Orientation of the light source is critical and humidity or atmospheric moisture is most difficult to arrange. It is, with light and air, an essential member of a trio.

Nevertheless, much ingenuity in extending window-sills into rooms and enclosing them, or opening windows outward into attached structures, has produced excellent results. For such projects, one would need certain prerequisites: lack of outdoor area; extraordinary impetus toward growing orchids; some construction and planning ability; and considerable patience. The finished job should compliment an interior and not detract from it. Similarly, any outdoor structure should be built or positioned in such a way as to not detract from the appearance of a garden. In this last instance, however, the light source for growing orchids—or any plants, for that matter—would be decisive.

CELLAR CULTIVATION

Cellars or basements are principally found in cooler to cold climates. Their modification for orchid growing entails much more than supplying light and warmth. In Australia cellar cultivation would be a novelty of some note, but in other countries, although perhaps uncommon, it is a way of life for some orchids and their growers.

In the *Orchid Review* (England) of September and October 1985, a grower in Canada outlined what apparently was a good conversion of a basement to orchid growing. Naturally there were no shade problems, but providing adequate light of the right colour was a major consideration. Other features were the isolation of the necessary humidity from the living area of the house, and careful selection of genera.

It would appear on a casual analysis that the plants would need to be of the lower strata type like paphiopedilums or phalaenopsis, rather than epiphytes from the upper natural strata. However, that could be modified to include some epiphytes if correct light, air flow and humidity were under control.

It is not possible to quote the whole of the article on basement cultivation, but the author had this to say of his experience:

I do not intend to give a list of those that 'do well under lights,' although I am aware of some that do not seem to work as well as others. I know it is true that some which have been failures under one grower's lights have done well under another's. Shouldn't we then classify this under 'Culture'? It may have been due to any of the other factors: type of light, intensity, length of days (species more so)—too long when they should have been short days, or vice versa—fertiliser, watering, etc. I have not been too successful with *Cattleya* Interglossa under lights, whereas in natural daylight in the greenhouse it would produce a beautiful 'bouquet' of eight or nine flowers. I also have experienced failures with equitant oncidiums which did well in the greenhouse. On the other hand I am having more success with paphiopedilums under lights and there is a very happy *Phragmipedium* Albopurpureum 'Grandiflora' just starting to bloom again. The first flower this year is just over 4½ inches across. Last year it produced nine flowers over a period of eight months.

At the beginning of this discussion I pointed out that one must always relate to the plants' needs as produced by their natural habitat. Many of us, including myself, try to grow plants requiring too wide a variety of conditions. Surely we can't be blamed for wanting to try. I do admire the person who has the will power to say 'no' and stick to only cool, medium or warm.

You may be able to play this game and win by having more than one growing area, each having a different temperature, and be the envy of those with only one greenhouse.

You may notice, when growing plants under lights, that they produce what appears to be an excessive amount of red pigmentation. This is the plant's built-in form of protection. They still continue to grow and produce flowers regardless.

Study your plants to try to determine whether you are giving them a suitable environment. If the growths are too long and trying to reach the light it would suggest that they need more. If, on the other hand, the leaves turn down as soon as possible to grow away from the light they are likely to be getting too much. These may display the excessive red pigmentation. A dark green plant tends to suggest that it is not getting enough light. A pale green or yellowish green plant is getting too much. Cattleyas, for example, while they may not look as appealing, usually produce more and better flowers if they are kept on the pale green side. An accordion-pleating effect in oncidiums, miltonias and related groups suggests that they need higher humidity.

It seems, from a consideration of the article, that this grower appeared to choose species orchids rather than hybrids, and that those plants from the lower strata, like paphiopedilums, were far easier to control.

Indoor growing of any type of orchid has little to recommend it except the sweet savour of success if it arrives. In general it could be claimed that while a glasshouse manager can with good cultural methods look forward to a plant life as long as his or her own, together with annual flowering, indoor cultivators of any genus must necessarily be patient and at times frustrated.

As far as growing orchids on window-sills or in living areas is concerned, it must be all or nothing, because very few orchids can live well or for long without a level of air flow and humidity which would play havoc with furnishings, wallpaper, and perhaps the health of the human components. In *Growing Orchids, Book One* there is an illustration of an indoor growing cabinet. It would be far better to construct a unit of this type than to try growing orchids in normal living areas.

In some books and journals it is common to find exhortations to 'grow your own orchids on your window-sill' or 'grow your own orchids in your bathroom' or some other place. But few if any of the writers have either tried it or persisted with it. To maintain under such conditions a cultural program to produce flowers— which is what orchid growing is all about—is too much to con- template. It is inconceivable to me as an orchid grower that anyone should base their plans on the short life which can be expected for orchids grown on window-sills or in bathrooms and the frequent replacement of the debilitated and killed-off stock. To do so is to treat these plants like so many other items of twentieth century obsolescence.

Where natural daylight cannot be used, plants must be grown under lights. Horticultural lighting used for indoor or artificial cultivation is almost exclusively fluorescent and the correct coloured tubes most frequently go under the name of Grolux. These should be mixed with either soft white or soft pink, colours which are occasionally dictated by the genera to be grown. Changes of colour should not be made at intervals of less than twelve months, unless the plants indicate by poor colour or growth that they are unsuited.

Probably indoor orchid growing, if it succeeded, would be the peak of specialist growing. Any success would depend largely on correct selection of genera. If possible the selection should be based on moist climate orchids for an indoor cabinet or hardier things which could spend part of their lives outdoors and be brought indoors for the flowers.

The moist-growing orchids which suggest possibilities are Slippers, masdevallias or phalaenopsis. Each of these needs different conditions, particularly masdevallias, some of which are warm growing and others suitable for intermediate to cool growing conditions.

If this is the way of life for a beginner, a lot of advice should be sought before money is spent on plants. As far as the cabinet itself is concerned, it must be constructed from waterproofed timber or metal, and considerable attention given to ventilation and humidity controls. There is little scope for beginners in the pastime ever to reach specialist standards with such equipment.

In concluding this review of indoor or basement cultivation, it should be again pointed out that it is a poor attitude to adopt when selecting plants for any system of growing, particularly species orchids, that a limited life should be proposed for them, even as a remote possibility.

There could be no greater contrast in orchid growing than to compare plants cultivated under lights to collections that are grown outside in natural conditions. It is not necessary to go to sub-tropical or tropical regions in order to grow orchids outdoors. For seventeen years I grew a specialist collection entirely on casuarina trees in what could be termed a less than temperate region. Two factors helped: closeness to the sea and the fortunate coincidence that the garden was in a small pocket which never had the frosts that occurred as short a distance away as two or three hundred metres. Again it was a matter of choosing the orchids which would be suited by the prevailing annual climate, and there were only two or three selections which failed to thrive and flower. To give some idea of the softness of the climate, it was possible to grow and flower *Dendrobium nobile* (Thunberg) and some of the less extended hybrids derived from it.

Orchids are frequently grown outdoors in those parts of Australia which support such types of culture, particularly in the north of the continent, where open and bush-house culture of all sorts of orchids is the norm. But these growers cannot grow the softer things like Slippers and odontoglossums without as much trouble as it takes a southern Australian to grow phalaenopsis.

Everything about orchid growing, and particularly specialist growing, is relative to specific areas of climate. If this is understood and acted on, it makes the pastime much simpler and more enjoyable.

SHADE

Few climates provide elementary conditions which allow glass-house growing without some form of shading to prevent sunburn. Nature provides its own shade and any orchid seeds which germinate and grow naturally depend in most instances on other plants and trees to provide shade for them. If they have never been seen by interested growers cultivating the plants artificially, some imagination is needed to visualise them in their natural surroundings. Occasionally imported plants give away some information which is totally lacking in artificially produced seedling plants. Small leaves and dwarfed pseudo-bulbs of natural plants could indicate that such plants had been collected from exposed positions in bright light. They should have been better developed and may have had little shade in their habitat. In artificial, well-adjusted conditions they may change their shape or morphology, as it is termed.

In nature, of course, those plants unfortunate enough to have lacked protection or those which lose their protection are soon casualties to climate. Most organisms are dependent on their environment, and on the ecology or grouping of organisms for mutual protection. In most instances cultivated plants lose many of their natural immunities because they are too well protected.

Artificial shade should be considered in association with other things such as duration and brightness of light, and the aspect or orientation of enclosures. However, it is scarcely worthwhile considering the nature of sunlight in different places because of the complexities involved. Sunlight has a definite quality and in passing it is worth noting that cymbidium plants grown in one area and transported to another with no apparent change in the sunlight may suffer burnt foliage. Such an instance is the difference between Sydney and Melbourne in Australia: cymbidiums grown in Sydney show much more light tolerance than those grown in Melbourne.

This demonstrates the fact that there are no rules which can be stated for shading of orchids either in the open or in enclosures. The amount of shade necessary to grow each genus in a particular location must be an individual decision based on experience. It may appear to be a bit rough on the plants, to subject them to the whims of climate in order to decide how much shade they need, but there is no other way. It should not be taken to extremes.

Means of providing shade have changed during the history of orchid growing. The old method of painting the glass still has advantages which are not shared by the most sophisticated woven plastic material. The effect sought is diffusion of sunlight, not elimination. Paint diffuses light, but it does not reduce it much: the effects may not suit all cultivated genera in mixed collections.

Paint should be applied in stages as seasonal change demands, and then removed in stages as sunlight moderates in other seasons. This, of course, means it must be water soluble and removable and not of the type used for house painting, whether acrylic or oil.

Lime was originally used as a wash and when mixed with 75 per cent water and 25 per cent milk it became waterproof to a degree and deteriorated sufficiently to weather off slowly. By autumn or when required, a light brush over with a wet broom removed all but an unimportant smear. But the lime wash had a disadvantage: it occasionally loses odd patches, through which moving sunlight could burn orchid foliage and cause disfigurement. This shading method would be only a last resort in the late years of this century.

Internal house paints, water soluble, were at one time frequently used to paint glasshouses. One enterprising manufacturer especially formulated a glasshouse paint which performed reasonably well, although on occasions the residue was hard to remove if almost clear glass was sought in dull months of the year. Paint is still worth considering for shading the side walls of glasshouses in preference to synthetic fabrics.

Plastic or synthetic fabrics were not the first to be used for shading. Hessian, a light brown open-weave fabric, was always popular when it was relatively cheap, particularly in preference to the somewhat cumbersome and heavy wooden lath blinds so frequently used. Hessian was woven from jute, the fibrous residue of *Cochorus capularis*, a tropical plant grown for the purpose, principally in India.

The relative merits of hessian placed it fairly high in comparison with most sophisticated weaves presented in the 1980 decade. It was available in grades, the lightest mesh of which would give something approaching a true 50 per cent shade. Lasting qualities of hessian, however, are poor compared with the synthetic cloth weaves. These synthetic weaves have improved in quality as experience of their deficiencies became apparent, and they should be usable for many years provided they are properly secured.

Most manufacturers give a shade figure for their weaves which is based on the amount of light reduction which occurs at a fixed distance from the cloth in full sunlight. It is not always a good guide in a universal sense, particularly for orchid growers. Experience

Soft-cane dendrobiums derived from Indo-Asian species were described in *Growing Orchids, Book Three* and are not included in this book. However, they are cultivated easily in sub-tropical and tropical climates under part-structures such as this and preferably with some protection in flowering.

is the best guide and the plants usually show by leaf colour and dehydration rate if it is sufficient. Information is also given on the subject in the other books *Growing Orchids, Books One, Two, Three* and *Four*.

As a matter of interest, in Melbourne two layers of 50 per cent shade cloth, one green and one black, give an exact reading of 50 per cent shade when measured with an ordinary photographic light meter held about 1 metre (just over 3 feet) below a glasshouse roof. This will convey some idea of the relevance of manufacturers' figures when a recommendation is made to use 50 per cent shade over some orchids. Two layers of 50 per cent shade cloth do not provide total shade in open sunlight or through clear glass, but something between only 50 to 60 per cent at the most. This information is more important in controlling climates of enclosures than may appear at first sight.

Shade is also related to the direction of sunlight in positioning enclosures. The ideal situation is with the structure running north and south for most genera, with full sunlight available from as close to sunrise as possible. *Growing Orchids, Book One* features various designs. Two are repeated in this volume, particularly with regard to designs which are the next best thing to north–south structures. Some orchid genera are better suited by either of these two designs than by the usual north–south orientation.

Most of the recommendations here are applicable to temperate climates rather than those of sub-tropical and tropical regions, which are dealt with below. It is possible to modify the temperate equation to suit any climate. Basic construction becomes a principal consideration, with shade following as a subsidiary to roof and wall design.

Although the principal consideration of this book is the housing of specialist collections, any orchid collection should have similar design so that if it is decided to grow other genera (within reason) then the basics are there to accommodate them.

IN THE TROPICS

Tropical regions have as much need for climate control as cooler temperate areas, and control begins in design and construction. It would be impossible to grow orchids in the tropics in the type of glasshouse common to cooler areas without using full air-conditioning, which would be prohibitively expensive. Even if air-conditioning were provided, a more careful selection of genera would be needed than for cool-climate cultivation. Probably the whole thing would prove unworkable because of poor growth and flowering.

Orchid growing in warm regions presents as many problems as in cool climates, but the cost of maintaining warmth does not enter into the program. Most structures are similar to this with shade-cloth the principal protection, preferably with metal mesh for support and strength. Construction costs are similar to those of structures in cool areas, because the roof must be at least partly protective.

The Paphiopedilum are usually regarded as plants for cultivation in intermediate to cool climates, those in the illustration were grown at McKinney's Nursery in Brisbane, Australia, in what could be best described as a sub-tropical climate.

The author can remember seeing a Slipper collection in Brisbane in the 1940s which had been brought from southern Australia, together with the methods used there for their cultivation. The project failed.

The secret of growing any orchids in most climates is waiting to be found by studying the modifications necessary to convert natural environments to stages where they become suitable for those orchids.

In the period since that 1940 decade the hybrid Slipper has changed but little. The final realisation of the desired shape has occurred and it is possible to use cross-pollinations to bring it to life almost at will.

However, in the lapse of forty years the needs of orchid growers have changed and they have obviously suffered a reversion in which the emphasis became stabilised on species and primary hybrids which were the original plants their ancestors grew. The trend has not been confined to Slippers alone. We have travelled the full circle and the casual or outside observer could well wonder at the lessons so well portrayed here.

There are still some achievements waiting in this bicentenary period of cultivation of the genus, with colour the principal focus. But for the specialist most desires have been fulfilled and the genus is so well understood that cultivation in sub-tropical and even tropical climates is possible.

A gallery of Phalaenopsis. An illustration of this collection in flower appeared in the winter, 1986, issue of the *Australian Orchid Review*. This is perhaps the ideal way to grow the genus because the plants have their foliage hanging naturally and all the spikes are displayed and free from each other. This collection of Mary Riordan, Innisfail, North Queensland, offers an ideal example for specialist phalaenopsis culture.

Phalaenopsis stuartiana (Reichenbach f.). Named in 1881 from material collected by Boxall from Agusan, in the Philippine Islands. Helen Valmayor in the model for orchid books, *Orchidiana Philippiniana*, states that it should have been credited to Boxall and not Stuart Low, after whom Reichenbach finally named it.

Phalaenopsis hybrids, like cymbidiums in cooler climates, can be used to good effect in mass displays. The colour range generally is through purple to rose to whites, but there is sufficient variation to create the rainbow. This display was assembled by Fame Orchids, of Brisbane, Australia, at the 10th Australian Orchid Conference at Adelaide in 1986.

Enclosures in the sub-tropics and tropics should be planned to give maximum air flow, while at the same time providing adequate control over the predators common to warm climates. Open-weave material sides ensure this, and with improved shade-cloth weaves their lifespan has been increased. The impervious wires like bronze and stainless steel have become too dear and are beyond the pockets of most growers.

Roofing has considerable effect on interior climates. It seems difficult but not impossible to obtain both durability and protection in the one roofing material. Plastic or fibre-glass corrugated roofing have short term durability compared with glass but they are almost a necessity for the tropics. The colour of roofing material should be a consideration, and the positioning of enclosures also has significance with this type of roofing. Preferably construction should ensure that the corrugations run north and south, irrespective of the colour used.

A good combination, when using plastic or fibre-glass roofing, is to alternate sheets of semi-opaque and green, so that as the sunlight moves across the plants a variation of intensity occurs. As pointed out in *Growing Orchids, Book Three*, page 65, if this design is followed it is possible also to use corrugated aluminium sheeting to reduce the light further. It may be necessary to slit the aluminium sheets lengthwise and narrow them so that the dark bands are not too broad.

Some sense could be made of a suggestion to avoid blue sheeting, but good orchid growing has also been reported when using this colour.

Whatever combinations are chosen, the effect on interior climate is considerable. Semi-opaque or clear fibre-glass or synthetic roofing overall would probably need some form of additional shading.

Roofs of corrugated plastic or fibre-glass may be used in sub-tropical and temperate climates, but for the latter they would need some modification to counteract over-ventilation where the corrugations meet at the apex of the roof. In fact, the same gaps could be entry points for pests in any climate, regardless of the better air flow necessary in sub-tropical or tropical regions.

In warm regions orchids may be grown in bush-houses. These are generally constructed with flat roofs, mostly with piping for support and roofing. The advantages of living in suitable climates are quite obvious if viewed from the construction and maintenance angle.

It should be remembered, however, that the micro-climates ordinarily associated with total enclosures almost disappear in structures with open-weave sides or totally open sides, and

Bringing your orchids into close contact with everyday living and the family, instead of isolating them in a separate enclosure, makes the pastime much more enjoyable. This is the author's set-up, the fourth which he has had in his lifetime.

The glasshouse is a prefabricated model removed from the previous site and re-erected. These prefabricated structures are accurately designed and drilled for easy erection and dismantling. The re-erection was done in one day. The structure is on the north side at the rear of the house and has two layers of shade-cloth to protect the plants.

The skillion-roofed section in the background is attached to a covered concrete area 8½ metres by 4½ metres, half of which is covered in shade-cloth and the other with Alsinite (alternating sheets of green and translucent), which gives 6½ metres by 4½ metres of space enclosed on all sides but the east. The windows at the rear of the house look out on to this area, which gets the sun almost from sunrise.

Plants from the glasshouse, when in flower, may be brought into such a protected area, provided the weather is not too cold, and add to the whole atmosphere of the working-dining area of the house.

Fibro-cement sheet is an excellent material for the tops of benches, because it does not rot or warp. It must be adequately supported. But it always seems to be manufactured in sizes that are not quite right.

If the proper tool for cutting it is not available the same job can be done efficiently with an ordinary hand saw. First clamp a batten along the line of the proposed cut; reverse the blade of the saw and using the first couple of teeth score a line alongside the batten. Two or three runs along the line are usually sufficient to groove it deeply enough to break. Remove the batten, put it under the sheet not quite to the break line and press firmly on each side of the scored line to obtain a clean break. I seem to remember, too, that it is best to measure twice and cut once.

temperature is almost constant from floor level to roof. But as there would be a small amount of relief at absolute floor level it should be taken advantage of and suitable plants grown there. Perhaps there is little scope for many of the softer cool-growing genera, but there is every reason to try growing paphiopedilums in even the most trying climates, and a modification for this level is mentioned in a later chapter.

The aim is always to use the capacity of various structures to the greatest advantage. Orchid growing in a specialist sense being what it is, the grower must carefully combine plants, climate and equipment.

Interior climates can be modified only within certain limits which are imposed by what goes on outside the enclosures. In cold climates it is necessary to supply warmth. This can be done by radiation from some form of heater or preconditioned air can be introduced. Both have limits beyond which plants deteriorate or are dehydrated too quickly. Much depends on the temperature range of each genus, which is not inflexible but has a great deal to do with successful specialisation.

Interior climates can also be cooled relative to unfavourable outside conditions. Shade plays an initial role, but must not be so dense that growth and flowering are affected. Evaporation may be used to cool the structure; this may be done by means of forced air circulation which picks up water vapour through air-permeable screens. Evaporative screens may be constantly saturated hessian

Growing orchids with a poor heat tolerance in a small glasshouse can be an unhappy experience, particularly when the structure is positioned to get adequate sunlight. The burden of heat on the plants may be reduced by an evaporative cooler such as this. They are frequently advertised cheaply, but make sure it is constructed of plastic and not metal, and that the water reservoir is also plastic. Make sure also that any appliance connected to the house electricity supply is correctly wired by a licensed electrical contractor or electrician.

or other open-weave materials, or composed of compressed straw. Any form of air-conditioner may be used provided it introduces wet air or water vapour, otherwise dehydration may occur and cause plant damage. Units which hold some hours' supply of evaporative water are freely available and, while not as effective as wet screens, they do the job quite well.

The most rudimentary evaporative coolers consist of shallow water containers over which air is forced by a fan. A certain amount of moisture is picked up, some of it condenses out on the foliage and contents of an enclosure as in the sophisticated forms. It is again evaporated from all surfaces and carries away certain amounts of unwanted heat. This is the basic theory and practice of cooling, depending only on air flow and suitable reservoirs of water over which the air is forced.

It must be appreciated at the outset that the tropical climates considered here are taken to be those in which at certain seasons of the year high temperatures are associated with high humidity, in which so long as there is an air flow the plants are benefited. In tropical but dry climates the moisture must be supplied and as much as possible left behind for the plants to pick up and use. The system is not easy to devise in shade-cloth enclosures and some form of automatic misting device must be used, or else a frequent hosing down or watering of the lower surfaces of the enclosure.

An automatic misting system is illustrated and explained in *Growing Orchids, Book Two*. This system is actuated by a timing device which automatically opens valves. Another device is illustrated in *Growing Orchids, Book One*. The actuating control is a counterbalanced mesh 'leaf' which operates an electrical control to turn on the water when it becomes dry, and closes off the watering system when it becomes misted and saturated. If anything, both are fallible and *do not provide suitable control over the moisture content of plant containers*.

Climate and shade are not the beginning and end of specialist cultivation, but they are closely related. If shading is too dense, evaporation is slowed down; if it is too light, evaporation is speeded up to a degree where there is no balance in the growing area and the changes become too fast for orchid plants to tolerate. *Stability is the secret of the whole exercise, however it may be reached.*

Each genus in specialist selection has its own particular point of stability and this was roughly expressed in the first pages of the book as cool, intermediate, and warm. Although we seek stability, it is not completely constant, but fluctuates in its character through the varying seasons of the year in a strict relationship with the region in which the plants are grown.

CHOOSING THE MAIN GENUS

Growers may be forced to exclude certain species from their program, and sometimes this follows the bitter experience of seeing plants deteriorate to a stage where they are no longer worth persisting with. We are not discussing here those growers fortunate enough to have unlimited resources to modify conditions to suit all genera.

The climate outside the glasshouse or enclosure should dictate the choice of plants. But instead of being the first point at issue it is frequently the last. Few orchid growers, experienced or not, are content to grow genera which they dislike, although possibly they cannot give a sufficiently good reason for that.

It has been my experience as a grower that I have liked any genus which I was able to grow successfully, and did not favour those which did not grow well for me. I would not be alone in that. Perhaps I listened to reason, but in the orchid-growing years I have lost count of the number of genera which had a place on the benches. In particular the genus phalaenopsis, beautiful as it is, has never been one which I chose to grow. This was partly because only a restricted choice of genera may be grown with it in the same glasshouse. All my orchid growing was in a temperate to cool climate and never in tropical conditions where mixing the warm-growing genera is much easier. The species *Phalaenopsis schilleriana* (Reichenbach f.) and *Phal. amabilis* (Linnaeus) failed to convert me to the genus, although they grew and flowered moderately well. As I cannot afford to have prejudices, principally owing to the position I have created for myself, I cannot say I dislike phalaenopsis simply because I have not been able to grow them. They failed to qualify because of the climate in which I grew orchids.

But enough of personal angles. We will stay with phalaenopsis for a little longer. On economic grounds these orchids should not be chosen as a specialist genus in a collection grown in a cool to cold climate, unless you can afford heating to maintain a *basic minimum* annual temperature of 15 to 18 degrees Celsius (60 to 65 degrees Fahrenheit). They do not depend on bright light like some other epiphytes because they are bred from species which in general are mid-range between floor-level plants and the lower epiphytes.

The *ideal for phalaenopsis hybrids* to upward of ten generations or most species is to have an enclosure shade conditioned to suit them. It should have a high permanent level of warmth between 22 and 28 degrees (about 70 to 80 degrees Fahrenheit), well-maintained humidity and a good air movement. The latter is necessary to prevent formation of disease spots on the foliage or flowers, so common a feature of poor conditions.

Other genera which will tolerate this are few and they depend principally on the restricted micro-climates such conditions offer. Phalaenopsis and associated orchids are essentially orchids for warmer climates.

No doubt most growers have had the experience of noting names in catalogues issued by suppliers of plants from all over the world that they would like to import to associate with phalaenopsis and other such orchids. Many have also been frustrated about importing and losing them through various quarantine procedures. It is seldom realised that orchids from tropical centres are the poorest travellers and slowest to acclimatise. At times this is the fault of suppliers dispatching plants during the wrong season, when they are at their sappiest and with new growths. They should arrive at their destinations in the warmest part of the year.

Orchid plants in their habitat, wherever it may be, suffer many of the disabilities and diseases they normally contract in cultivation, and it would be wrong to imagine that a natural plant is always strong and healthy. Mostly they are much 'tattier' than their cultivated kin.

The difference to be expected from phalaenopsis and other tropical genera grown in natural warm climates compared with those grown in temperate and cooler climates would be in the development of the plants, length of the flower racemes, the number and size of flowers and general lasting quality. For this reason it is recommended that they should be the choice of people in suitable climates. They are not for 'triers', because they have been tried many times without much success.

There are innovations such as hybrids developed between sarcochilus and phalaenopsis, particularly *S. hartmannii* (Mueller). This branch is still in the formative stages and it may not be until a few more generations that a 'phalaenopsis' will be developed which will withstand quite cool temperatures to satisfy the specialist desires of those who live in such climates. The development is very promising.

When grown in their correct environment phalaenopsis may be combined well with cattleyas, dendrobiums of the phalaenanthe or spathulate sections and many other orchids suitable for sub-tropical and tropical culture.

It would be wrong to leave the genus without some indication of the sort of climate which would be ideal for its cultivation. Although it may be difficult to indicate with accuracy the absolute limits, a suitable climate should not have a long, dull season in the dryer or cooler months of the year. The real growing period should be of no less duration than six months, with *few if any recessions into temperatures lower than 15 degrees Celsius.* Back-up equipment to ameliorate the conditions on these occasions would be a necessity.

Phalaenopsis may be grown in quite cold natural climates if under glass and preferably within a *temperature minimum* of about 15 to 18 degrees. The deficiencies of such cultivation have been noted when flowering is taken into account. It may be thought that the temperatures quoted are wide, but it should be remembered that the basic minimum of 15 degrees is absolute while the upper and middle ranges are quite flexible.

3 CYMBIDIUMS

Many specialist growers base their collections on this genus, and it can be rewarding in cold, temperate and lightly sub-tropical climates. Best results appear to come from zones where summer temperatures fluctuate between 15 and 27 degrees Celsius (about 60 to 80 degrees Fahrenheit) and with *winter minimum* of about 10 degrees Celsius (about 50 degrees Fahrenheit). The critical requirement for these orchids appears to be the reduction of the temperature in early autumn and through winter, with a lift to the upper limits in late spring. Cymbidiums have much to offer in these climates because it is possible to have clones flowering as early as May and a progression of flowers until about the beginning of November in standard hybrids. Intermediate and miniature clones may produce flower through the blank period.

If anything could be held against the genus it would be the inability of growers to maintain a static collection for any length of time. While it is possible to bench a collection of cattleyas good for all time in regard to quality and general appreciation, the cymbidium world is in constant change. In many instances the newcomers are little different from those they supplant and everything depends on the method of appreciation, which is not confined to beauty alone. Relegation of clones is continuous and not confined to any one country and apparently in the eyes of some beholders it must be new to be good.

The specialist should not be swayed by such opinions, but should continue to produce quality and satisfaction from cymbidiums as old as comparative genera such as cattleyas.

A better understanding of the genus has enabled growers in lower sub-tropical regions to grow cymbidiums, particularly close to the coast or at altitudes of some 300 to 900 metres (about 1000 to 3000 feet). However, in these areas cymbidiums as a main genus

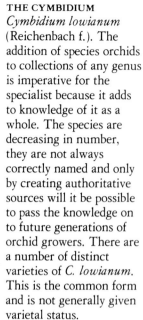

THE CYMBIDIUM
Cymbidium lowianum
(Reichenbach f.). The
addition of species orchids
to collections of any genus
is imperative for the
specialist because it adds
to knowledge of it as a
whole. The species are
decreasing in number,
they are not always
correctly named and only
by creating authoritative
sources will it be possible
to pass the knowledge on
to future generations of
orchid growers. There are
a number of distinct
varieties of *C. lowianum*.
This is the common form
and is not generally given
varietal status.

Cymbidium lowianum
var. *Concolor*. The source
of most of the self-
coloured hybrids many
generations removed from
this species form. Its first
notable hybrid was
Cymbidium President
Wilson, known also as the
variety 'Concolor', which
is still cultivated by
discerning specialists.
*Growing Orchids, Book
One*, contains other
illustrations of cymbidium
species.

31

Cymbidium parishii var. *sanderae* (Reichenbach f.). This flower is reproduced from a contemporary illustration in the *Gardeners' Chronicle.* The *Orchid Review* for June 1904 gives a description, from which it is obvious that some mericlones sold as *C. parishii* var. *sanderae* in the 1980 decade were incorrectly labelled. The true species never carried more than two to five flowers. It has been considered conspecific with *C. eburneum,* which if accepted could create havoc with *Sander's List of Orchid Hybrids*.

Cymbidium parishii. This is a 4n conversion of *C. parishii,* but it is not entitled to the varietal name *sanderae.* The original clone *C. parishii* var. *sanderae* was lost to cultivation, but the species generally survived.

32

Cymbidium Tommy 'Amy'. The principal member of the genus responsible for much of the beauty of miniature species in hybrid form is *C. pumilum* (Rolfe), and it could not be better represented than by this magnificent specimen exhibited at the 10th Australian Orchid Conference in Adelaide, South Australia, in 1986.

Cymbidium erythrostylum (Rolfe), a Vietnamese species which was cross-pollinated with other species and hybrids to make use of its early-flowering capabilities. With considerable patience, hybridists corrected its undesirable flower formation within some six generations without losing the early-flowering characteristic.

33

Cymbidium Jubilation
(*C.* Borough Green x
C. Wallara) was featured
in *Growing Orchids, Book
One*, giving its pedigree
and dealing with apparent
discrepancies in the
breeding. This is a
different clone, carrying
the varietal name
'Geronimo'.

The clone 'Geronimo'
was accorded an unusual
honour in the history of
the genus in Australia
because it gained a First
Class Certificate.

The art of specialising

in this 1980 decade has
been made much easier
with the introduction of
mericloning. Collections
can now be improved
more quickly, and it is
common to note these
first quality orchids in the
groups of plants beginners
or novices use as
commencement points
of their careers in the
pastime. However, it
should not be thought that
by buying these clones
success is assured. The
grower must still solve the
basic cultural problems,

limit the numbers of
plants, and determine the
suitability of their
environment.

C. Jubilation was
selected as the most
appropriate orchid to
illustrate the ultimate of
which the genus was
capable in *Book One*. The
honours accorded, a First
Class Certificate from the
Victorian Orchid Club and
later the Australian Orchid
Council, have confirmed the
opinion originally formed.

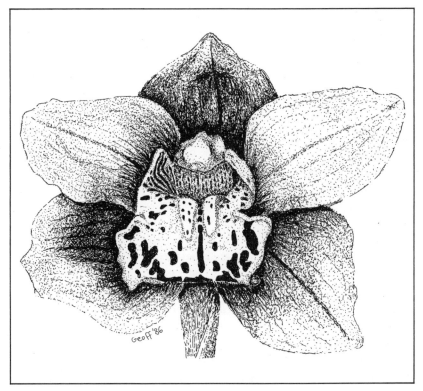

Cymbidium Fanfare
The bicentenary years of orchid growing introduced two new features to cymbidium hybrids in the dramatic increase in size of the flowers and the ease of propagation by the meristem system.
C. Fanfare is quite large at 12·5 centimetres (about 5 inches), very solid in substance and green with bronze tinges. (A Geoffrey Skilbeck ink drawing)

in some years should be expected to go thoroughly wrong, particularly in specialist cultivation. The problem is principally caused by radical weather patterns and sometimes occurs in the best growing areas.

In general these orchids are well suited to realistically changing weather patterns, but the changes must be within the limits given above if you are looking for the ultimate the genus can produce by ordinary good growing. Forcing the plants and flowers is something that must be paid for.

If the climate is suitable for cymbidiums, woven synthetic fabrics of fairly light quality from 50 per cent upward provide almost sufficient protection from direct sunlight for most days of the year, provided the foliage is kept dry. For perfectionist growing and flowering, more protection from both wind and weather would be needed from apparent bud stage onward, to prevent bud and flower abrasion.

For those wanting more information on the genus there are numerous publications including *Growing Orchids, Book One*. Modern hybrids were developed from several species originating in India, Burma and other Indo-Asian countries, and most are reproduced in Book One.

In their development modern hybrids have undergone a lot of

mutation and controlled alteration, and a quick comparison with the species will indicate the metamorphosis of the genus in modern hybrids.

As a family these orchids are most suitable for easy cultivation as well as specialist handling, to both of which may be attributed the hold they have in many countries over orchid-growers, and have had for some eighty years.

The stability of the pastime was upset by the introduction of the meristem process of propagation. It opened up new fields and made distribution of quality clones simpler and quicker than by ordinary propagating methods. While many growers may resent the advent of the process because they are forced to keep up with the times, the specialist should not be so affected. Any replacement of the original intended collection will only be through the discard of an entire stock of any clone because a better one has been produced.

The balance in flowering remains essentially the same, with perhaps up to five years between flowerings which are the ultimate of any clone. The specialist should respect this fact and realise that weather patterns, annual cycles and plant maturity are almost beyond control. He or she will try to minimise the effect of these factors to a degree by growing at least two and preferably three plants of the better clones, trying to rotate their handling and flower production, and above all understanding the habit of plants to flower on new growth or old.

The absolute best from any clone is usually attained by correct handling, reducing the number of flowers to a preferable number by good cultivation and correct fertilising without forcing. It is specialist technique exemplified and not easy to maintain.

As this book was being written the problem of virus in the genus continued, accentuated perhaps by the mericloning process. The latter was also possibly responsible for some of the foliage damage usually associated with virus but which may prove, with sufficient investigation, to be a parallel non-virus manifestation. It was hard to separate the two and this in turn led to misinformation and misunderstanding. Mericloning, for all its facility and value, apparently has a lot to answer for. Some of it is apparent in the colour illustrations 'Where Did We Go Wrong' and further explained there. I believe nearly all cymbidium plants carry latent virus.

Quite separate from the standard size cymbidiums, those bred for small neat plants are most suitable for a main genus when space is a consideration. Two distinct types are common. The smallest, known as the miniature cymbidium, is bred from naturally small species. The second category, known as an intermediate type cymbidium, is principally the result of cross-pollination between standard size clones and true miniature species or hybrids. In many instances these intermediate cymbidiums are little better than types which were culled from collections in the middle years of cymbidium cultivation about the late 1940s. In general the miniatures and intermediates which are worth a place in specialist collections are a minority of the total in a true assessment of these sections of the genus.

The true miniatures fall into two types: those which have pendant spikes, and those with erect or semi-erect flower spikes. The ones with pendant flower spikes may cause a space problem: the spikes are produced in profusion on mature plants, and the specimens must be suspended rather than benched in the normal way so that the racemes can grow and be arranged to the best advantage. Very few miniature plants which naturally develop pendant spikes can be handled to convert them to erect stance. The plants should be rotated through a full circle each week so that all the flower spikes can develop naturally. This is best done as soon as they are noticed, at whatever time of the year.

An excellent example of cultivation to specialist standards using miniature *Cymbidium* Tommy 'Amy' appears in the illustrations.

If erect flower spikes of most clones—miniature, intermediate or standard—are preferred there is one very simple way they can be controlled, although it may not always succeed with pendant spikes.

Most cymbidium spikes are soft until the buds begin to separate from the stem. Once there is room to move them slightly on a spike a rubber band, preferably thin and about 7 or 8 centimetres long (about 3 inches), should be looped about the stem between the second and third top buds on the spike. From an overhead support point another rubber band of the same elasticity should be also looped. There should preferably be about half to two-thirds of a metre between the two rubber bands. A light string is tied to the upper rubber band and passed through the loop of the lower one. Each day this string should be tightened a little, which stretches the spike erect and keeps it there. The buds may be positioned on the spike as they mature, but enthusiasm in this direction too soon has only one result.

This system works quite well, but do not put the rubber band around the stem of the uppermost bud or it will break off. It must be between the last two and three, and the whole operation handled very carefully. For specialist collections grown in carefully monitored space it offers total control over growing and flowering. If an arching flower spike is preferred, it may also be controlled in this way. Since cymbidium flowers and flower spikes grow more at

Flowers for exhibition, irrespective of genus, should be presented to display their full potential. In cymbidium growing the nature of some spikes prevents this, but the curved or arching habit of the inflorescence may be counteracted. As soon as the spike will withstand careful handling and while it is still sappy, a rubber band should be looped about the upper part of the spike between the second and third bud from the top. Immediately above the spike another rubber band should be looped from the roof or other support, and the two rubber bands joined by a lightly tightened piece of thin string. Each morning the string should be tightened to tension the rubber bands. If this is done consistently, the spike will be straightened and irrespective of the angle of view some fully opened flowers will appear face on. As the stem hardens the rubber band should be transferred from between the upper buds to the stem just below the top bud. Do not loop it around the pedicel of the flower and do not tension it too tightly or the top bud will snap off. Do not use heavy rubber bands, and perhaps make a trial run on something unimportant.

night than in daylight, the adjustment to the suspension is best made each morning.

Do not begin this training too soon and preferably do not try it once the spikes have begun to harden. The decision should be made considering the nature of the inflorescence and the length to which it may grow, and its pendant nature if it is a miniature.

While it would be possible to destroy any pleasure in the pastime by rigid attitudes, some hard decisions must be taken every time the collection flowers. They must all be worth the space they occupy, and the reasons for choice in the first place must have some weight. At times I have had to choose between a plant which flowers every year, sometimes twice on the same pseudo-bulb, and one which may be slightly better but is shy about flowering.

The proportion of plants which should flower under a well-planned system could probably never average more than 80 per cent, which is not too bad when compared with the usual average over a collection of about 50 per cent. In limited space the percentage is important.

To produce these flowers do not experiment too frequently. A fertiliser should be given at least two years to prove its worth, unless its deficiencies are obvious in the flowers of the first year of use. If it appears borderline it should be given a second chance.

One of the best fertilisers, proved over many years by reputable growers, is hoof and horn meal. It is relatively cheap, and easy to apply. It should be given in early October and again at the end of February, and can take the flowers through to late spike development, which is the stage just before the buds break out of the sheaths. After that, for the plants to give top-quality flowers, a good but weak booster is all that is needed. Do not be tempted to force the plants beyond their capability to flower and revive after that effort.

A soluble fertiliser such as Aquasol, with an NPK (nitrogen, phosphate and potash) rating of 23–4–18 is a good base. To two litres of water (about 3½ pints) add 125 grams (about 5 teaspoons) of Aquasol or similar fertiliser, about 25 grams (about 1 heaped teaspoon) of magnesium sulphate (Epsom salts), a similar amount of sulphate of iron and 100 millilitres (about 5 fluid ounces) of Maxicrop (seaweed fertiliser). Never try to guess the amounts and throw them in indiscriminately. Always measure the quantities and do not vary them unless you have some very good reason. The constituents should be thoroughly shaken until dissolved and used at the rate of 25 to 30 millilitres (about 3 level tablespoons) to an eight-litre bucket of water. About two cups of the diluted fertiliser should be enough for a 200 to 250 millimetre pot.

The concentration suggested may appear too weak to be effective, but most orchid growers overestimate the nutrient requirements of their plants. This mix is designed to be used every time the plants need water, and without the need to flush out the potting mix as appears so necessary with some fertilising methods. There are many other formulations about, but this one is proved and quite safe for cymbidium culture. Some may prefer different formulas, particularly in the matter of the iron content, but the sulphate is easily dissolved and available for the plant if needed.

When using any type of soluble inorganic fertiliser, make sure the plants are damp. Water them, if necessary, the day before the fertiliser is used. Do not be afraid to use the fertiliser in the evening in the growing and pre-flowering period, which is usually summer to early autumn. Do not be tempted to increase the quantity of liquid fertiliser beyond the proportion quoted, because the forcing stage is soon entered and causes root damage and subsequent foliage damage.

Most specialist growers work out their own fertiliser systems and it is not overstating the position to say that totally different fertilisers may be necessary and suitable in different climates.

Any collection of cymbidiums should include whatever species are available and as many varieties as can be fitted in. They should include: *Cymbidium eburneum* (Lindley), *C. erythrostylum* (Rolfe), *C. giganteum* (Lindley), *C. grandiflorum* (Griffith), *C. i'ansonii* (Lowe), *C. insigne* (Rolfe), *C. lowianum* (Reichenbach f.), and *C. tracyanum* (Rolfe).

These species are mentioned in *Growing Orchids, Book One* and are the basic material used in producing most of the 1980s hybrids. Their characteristics are directly traceable in all these cymbidiums through to the most complex of the cross-pollinations. There were other minor supposed natural hybrids which played some part in the colour lines, but they were noted in *Growing Orchids, Book One* and are not repeated here.

In cultivating species it will become obvious from which particular cymbidiums the habits of flowering on old or new growths will be understood. Of all the main species only *Cymbidium tracyanum* (Rolfe) has a minor part and that was because it indicated in such things as primary hybrids that the flowers had poor lasting qualities. The record flower life of six months belongs to *Cymbidium lowianum* (Reichenbach f.).

Some space should be allocated to addition of seedlings each year. They must fit into the plan and not take up the space devoted to the main collection. This applies also to additions of mericlone propagations bought to replace a main clone. All orchid growers tend to overuse the space available, but for a specialist this may be the first stage in a breakdown that becomes continuous and puts an end to the original idea.

Miniature species cymbidiums are not as easy to cultivate as the larger ones for a number of reasons, varying from needing slightly more warmth than standard species to the idiosyncrasies of the Australian trio, each one of which appears to need a different set of conditions and potting material to survive. However, each is worth the effort, success of which will depend on following the growing pattern and material in which they thrive naturally. *Cymbidium devonianum* (Paxton) has added richness of colour to the hybrid range and much of the success story of miniaturising the hybrid form of the genus must be attributed to the Chinese and Japanese forms of the species *Cymbidium pumilum* (Rolfe).

Cymbidium species growers should not take labels too seriously without complete investigation of basic data. In the 1980 decade several different forms of *Cymbidium parishii* var. *sanderae* were obtainable. There was only one original plant and it was lost from cultivation. The full history and description of this cymbidium was given in the *Orchid Review* of June 1904, by Robert Allen Rolfe, editor of that journal, and this version is the only one worth referring to. There were several depictions of the flower, two of which were accurate. That of John Day, figured in *The Orchid Album*, and the drawing which appeared in the *Gardener's Chronicle*, volume 2, of 1878 (page 74), are authentic and beyond dispute. A reproduction of the latter appears in the illustrations in the colour pages. An important point to note is the number of flowers carried by this species. It never had more than five flowers on the best of plants. They were 'ivory white with a pair of orange coloured crests on the lip, a yellow area in front and numerous large purple blotches nearer the margin'.

The clone which I flowered bore 11 flowers, was pinkish and bore no resemblance to the flowers which I saw in New South Wales before World War II, when most of the species cymbidiums were cultivated by a number of growers. The plants derived from American stock do not resemble these New South Wales plants, and it is quite wrong to have recognised any of the 4n derivatives as *Cymbidium parishii* var. *sanderae*.

Having been involved in growing and flowering the species cymbidiums from my earliest orchid-growing days, and also growing and flowering many primary and secondary hybrids, I had little trouble identifying the clone which I bought under this label. If *Cymbidium eburneum* (Lindley) and *Cymbidium parishii* (Reichenbach f.) are one and the same thing then it is *Cymbidium* Gottianum. But if they are separate species it is *Cymbidium* Dryad. The other parent in both instances is *Cymbidium insigne* (Rolfe) and there is no doubt whatsoever that my plant has this species in its immediate background. Both these hybrid cymbidiums appear in my records of plants which I flowered and both are imprinted on my memory.

The specialist should take a certain amount of pride in tracing some of the more important primary hybrids such as *Cymbidium* Lowio-eburneum (*C. lowianum* x *C. eburneum*) but disregarding modern remakes which have used colchicine-treated species to produce variables.

Several others should be included, namely, *Cymbidium* Alexanderi (*C.* Lowio-eburneum x *C. insigne*), *C.* Pauwelsii (*C. insigne* x *C. lowianum*), *C.* Lowio-grandiflorum (*C. lowianum* x *C. grandiflorum*), of which there are many plants about masquerading as *C. lowianum*; *C.* President Wilson (*C.* Alexanderi x *C. lowianum*), particularly the form 'Concolor'. *Cymbidium* Coningsbyanum (*C. insigne* x *C. grandiflorum*); and particularly *Cymbidium* Ceres (*C. i'ansonii* x *C. insigne*), which was the basis of much of the pink and red colouring of modern hybrids and has been taken to brilliance by line breeding some of the 1950 hybrids.

Cymbidium insigne cross-pollinated with *C. erythrostylum* produced *Cymbidium* Albanense in 1915, and this orchid may be most difficult now to find. It is one of the keys to the modern complex, particularly in the early flowering section.

In the lifetime of an orchid grower these may still be remembered by some of the older specialists, because they comprised major elements in specialist collections of the years between 1930 and 1945.

Some of the hybrids mentioned also included variables such as *Cymbidium* Alexanderi 'Westonbirt' and *C.* Pauwelsii 'Compte de Hemptinne' which were the building blocks of the cymbidium world as a whole. A specialist should be acquainted with these orchids if only in name. Unfortunately some of the orchid world vandals have subverted even these primary elements in our cult and converted them into monstrosities in a search for epoch-making new cymbidium hybrids.

The specialist would do well to disregard other than the genuine original clones if they are procurable, and leave out of collections those which have wrong-coloured labellums and other variations. Illustrations of the originals are available from various sources to verify their credentials. None of these primary or secondary hybrids are going to add glamour to a specialist collection, but they will add a touch of history and a talking point. It is almost certain that in the 1990s and onward they will also add intrinsic value, for what that should be worth to any self-respecting specialist.

POTTING MATERIALS

There have been few changes in recent years to the composition of the various mediums used in potting cymbidiums. A different mix which I have never advocated is described here. There are risks in its handling by inexperienced growers. It involves what for want of a better term could be called composting with unusual materials. I must stress that this potting mix should not be used for any orchids other than cymbidiums.

The quantities are as follows:

Four parts of hardwood sawdust and/or buzzer shavings.
One part of dry fowl manure. It is essential that it be dry, because otherwise it is apt to cake and remain undistributed through the mix.

THE PRODUCT IN THE 1980 DECADE
Cymbidium Winter Wonder (*C.* Winter Fair x *C.* Fanfare). One of the cymbidiums included to indicate the developments from the species. It could well be termed incredible that all this colour was hidden away in the genetic pool. This white is not the ultimate in shape but is included because of its *C. erythrostylum* antecedent.

Cymbidium Fury (*C.* Khyber Pass x *C.* Sensation). Although no cymbidium species carries much hint of this brilliance, it was developed from *Cymbidium* Ceres, which came from the cross-pollination of *C. i'ansonii* and *C. insigne* var. *sanderi*, which was pink, both of which were illustrated in *Growing Orchids, Book One*.

HYBRIDISING FAULTS

Where did we go wrong?
Cymbidiums such as this
are uncommon, but so
many minor faults occur
that a reason must be
there somewhere in our
methods. First, we have
bred a race of fault-bearing
stock, then unnaturally
reproduced copies with the
cloning process. There is
nothing else which can
carry the blame. It is there
now for all time unless a
fresh start is made.

Cymbidium Firevieux
(*C.* Firewheel x *C.* Vieux
Rose). There can be little
doubt that this unusual
and strangely beautiful
flower is the result of both
processes outlined above.
Has it a future? If so,
where does it lie? Can it
produce a new race of
cymbidiums? Can its
symmetry and colour
outweigh its deficiencies?
It is much easier to ask the
questions than to answer
them. There are a number
of these freak clones in
cultivation, all of them
beautiful.

44

One part of coarse sharp sand and/or fine gravel.

Allow half a cup of hoof and horn fertiliser or blood and bone fertiliser or a mix of the two to each bucket of mix.

The constituents should be barrowed on to a concrete slab and turned over thoroughly with a shovel in the dry state. The mix is then hosed thoroughly and turned over lightly so that it is moist right through without any excess water running from it. After hosing and turning again to make sure that the whole mix is thoroughly damp and integrated, it should be shovelled into a heap and preferably covered with a sheet of plastic or old plastic bags to keep the moisture in.

After two days the heap should be turned over again and again. It will be found that a certain amount of heat has been generated; if not, then the covering should be replaced and onset of heating awaited. The covering should always be replaced after turning. The heap should be turned over every second day for about a fortnight and by then most of the heat will have gone out of the mix.

Once the heat has gone, the mix is in the state where it may be used. It will be found much easier to work into cymbidium root systems than conventional mixes compounded with bark, charcoal or gravel, peanut shells and various other additives.

Do not try to grow part of your collection in this mix and another part in orthodox mixes, because the handling and watering systems are quite different. Watering of plants growing in this mix should be careful and infrequent, but as a growing medium it surpasses many others.

It is important to make sure that the sawdust is hardwood and not pine because pine sawdust could have come from treated pine and that would produce instant disaster. When you buy or obtain the sawdust, make sure that the supplier knows what it is to be used for, so there is less likelihood of a mistake.

If plastic pots are used they should have small holes in the bottom as well as slits in the sides. Drainage is doubly important with this compost: the cymbidium roots will penetrate right to the bottom because the moisture is retained there and not in the upper layers. The mix does not dry out as rapidly as common mixes.

If using terracotta pots they should be crocked more thoroughly than when using coarse mixes, and a light layer of porous vegetable material such as fern frond placed over the layer of crocks. Bracken fern is suitable for this, but it must be dry and only a scrim layer used. Treefern frond may be used in the same way but is probably less easy to get than bracken fern. Do not use green fronds of either.

Always enlarge the holes in the bottoms of terracotta pots. Small holes such as cut by manufacturers are more likely to block than when they are double the size.

Any fertiliser boosting should be approached with as much care as watering, and a year or two may be necessary to get the 'feel' of the system.

This potting mix is not new. It has been known and used for more than forty years. Originally the potting mix for cymbidiums was made up from turf peat, fibre and a certain amount of soil of a non-compacting type. The next move, as the number of people growing orchids increased and fibre became scarce, was to a potting mix based on tan-bark. This mix was again superseded when leather tanning processes changed and the acacia bark used in the older process became too difficult to get. As this book was being written pine bark is the base for a number of formulations, but it, too, is becoming expensive. The sawdust mix is not expensive and once 'seasoned' and inert it can be stored dry or almost dry for a long period. All that is necessary is care in handling it and the realisation that a different growing technique is needed.

Frequent repotting should be part of the specialist technique with cymbidiums—perhaps every second year—and with the sawdust mix this is less of a problem than with bark mixes. When repotting, the root system should be pruned of all doubtful sections and the root that may be left on spent pseudo-bulbs in the previous repotting. This is important. As this mix is very rich in cymbidium food there will be less root formed in the two-year period.

The plants should be prepared for repotting by drying out for as long as it takes and then carefully removing each plant from its pot by sliding it out on to a sheet of plastic. It will move more freely than when grown in bark mixes. The old mix will shake free quite easily and the root system should be fitted into a fresh pot, larger if necessary. Support the plant by holding the leaves when fitting it into the pot, and give scope for new growth by siting the plant toward the side.

If the plant appears too large to see out the following two years, carefully remove one or more of the older pseudo-bulbs, severing the rhizome with a very sharp sterilised knife or small saw.

This is the stage where knowing the habits of plants in flowering from new growth or older pseudo-bulbs is helpful. The general idea in repotting should be to keep the plants in flowering shape so that they do not miss a year. The plan is never perfect, but it should be kept in mind and worked on.

If it appears that the stage of growth is wrong for repotting, it may be best to leave the plant for another year and try to work in a replacement. It is not good practice, when using the sawdust mix, to pot plants on into the next sized pot. They should be stripped of all the old mix if they are disturbed.

A word of warning: It is inadvisable to use this potting material for other genera grown with a cymbidium collection. They should be grown in the standard potting mixes commonly used.

The principal aim in designing potting materials and fertiliser additives is not to produce more flowers on cymbidium spikes, but rather to reduce the number and concentrate on their quality. It is usual to attain this goal by propagating plants of about four or five mature pseudo-bulbs, well leafed, and producing at the most two flower spikes. If necessary remove additional flower spikes, but do not disbud them to promote size and quality.

It has been said with some truth that cymbidiums will grow in almost any medium. Frequently a change in medium is forced on growers by lack of supply, but innovation is a considerable portion of the pastime. Some growers have turned to materials which in the ordinary course of culture could be regarded as more than innovatory. One of these is horse manure, but the results are equal only to those which could be obtained with any other potting mix.

Naturally there are always retarding factors, and horse manure may be hard to get in your district. It cannot be recommended, for a number of reasons, but there is evidence that horse manure can be used successfully for the genus. It would need understanding, and it would be best to experiment with one or two plants not highly valuable to test its suitability for your climate and environment.

Any organic fertiliser, particularly the more odorous type, attracts earthworms. Earthworms fulfil important functions in agriculture, but are most unwelcome in cymbidium culture for two reasons—they destroy the nature and drainage of material in containers and I believe they are possible virus carriers. The point of infection is more likely to be through the root system than by any other means.

CYMBIDIUM COMPATIBLES

Considering the demands made by cymbidiums on space, any genus benched with them must be competitive and tall growing unless they are 'shelter' plants which do not mind overhanging foliage.

Cymbidiums are what could be termed dry growing, and other orchids chosen for combination should be seasonally tied to similar patterns of summer growth, autumn maturity and late winter or spring flowering. The range is considerable.

Occasionally particular orchids should be thought of as single-plant additions to cymbidium collections, but they should be worth-while and give flowers each year rather than be chance hopefuls. It is easy to be impressed by such plants as well-flowered masdevallias, which could be totally unsuitable. Admire but forget them and concentrate on other equally beautiful subjects which will fit into the scheme.

Australian orchids from temperate to sub-tropical zones, par-ticularly epiphytic species, should be ideal subjects. In some instances these would be found among dendrobiums rather than anything else. They have the qualifications because they may be benched or suspended.

Larger subjects such as *D. speciosum* (J. E. Smith) may prove problems, taking more space than fully grown cymbidiums. Others are *Dendrobium falcorostrum* (Fitzgerald), *D. adae* (Bailey), *D. aemulum* (Robert Brown), *D. kingianum* (Bidwill) in almost endless variation, *D. agrostophyllum* (F. Mueller), *D. ruppianum* (Hawkes) and members of the terete or pendulous group such as *D. beckleri* (F. Mueller). Then there are the smaller dendrobiums such as *D. linguiforme* (Swartz), all of which are best suited on slabs of various materials which can be hung against the walls.

Dendrobium speciosum (J. E. Smith). Two forms of this magnicent dendrobium, both from New South Wales. The uppermost plant came from the vicinity of Sydney, the other from a northern habitat. This is one of the world's most spectacular orchids. The author has seen some plants which are large enough to fill the tray of a one-tonne truck and having more than one hundred pseudo-bulbs. In its best presentations it is a specialist orchid. Each pseudo-bulb in its erratic flowering life may produce as many as ten spikes, frequently with two or three at a time on the pseudo-bulbs. It is not deciduous and the leaf life could be upward of ten years, depending on cultivation or in natural habitats on seasonal conditions.

Plants to avoid are tropical species such as *D. bigibbum* (Lindley). There are also good reasons for leaving out *D. tetragonum* (Cunningham) and taking instead some of the hybrids developed from it, such as *D.* Ellen, *D.* Hilda Poxon, *D.* Star of Gold and further generations. These hybrids are illustrated in *Growing Orchids, Book Four* and their value lies in the habit of flowering almost continuously throughout the year.

A feature to look for in choosing these—and for that matter any other compatible orchids—is the way they can be used to grow against walls at the sides or ends of enclosures so that they do not overhang the principal genus.

There is reason to doubt the value or reliability of *Dendrobium fleckeri* (Rupp and White) as a cymbidium associate, but some of the hybrids to which it contributes, such as *D.* Peach Glow, *D.* Wonga and further generations are beautiful and compatible in cool climates. Most of these dendrobiums are spring flowering and summer flowering genera are few.

Zygopetalums are similar to cymbidiums. While the selection available may not be large, it would be no trouble to carry two or three plants of *Z. mackayi* (Hooker), which is autumn flowering, or *Z. crinitum* (Loddiges), which is spring flowering. *Z. mackayi* has a confused background and some plants which carry the name are in dispute. It has been confused with *Z. intermedium* (Loddiges), as the difference between the two is no more than occurs in varieties of species in other genera. The taxonomic discussion is not worth the trouble.

Z. mackayi (Hooker) flowers on the new growths, the plants are easily grown and the same compost or potting mix as for cymbidiums is adequate, *but do not use the sawdust mix for any orchids other than cymbidiums.*

Zygopetalums generally dislike very cold weather and the foliage usually indicates by developing black spotting and patches that they are growing in borderline conditions. It is disfiguring and when taken to extremes may affect the whole plants. The leaves should be kept as dry as possible during winter or colder periods of the year.

The value of these orchids is that they may be grown under the same program as cymbidiums, with fully developed plants capable of carrying two spikes on each new pseudo-bulb and mature plants producing as many as six or more spikes on a 25-centimetre pot of *Z. mackayi*. *Zygopetalum crinitum* (Loddiges) is equally productive.

A number of attractive hybrids have been developed from *Z. mackayi* (Hooker). Some of these hybrids carry shorter spikes and fewer flowers than the species parent, but the colour has been intensified by using well-coloured forms. In some instances this has been taken to deep purple tints, which on a green base colour gives a very good impression. Two of these were shown in *Growing Orchids, Book Two* where other zygopetalums were also featured.

Reference should be made to that book for general culture, also to Orchidaceae Brasilienses, by Pabst and Dungs, for illustrations of other species. Not all these associates would be suitable for this section of cymbidium collections.

Such a minor collection as an assembly of zygopetalums must be carefully handled so that it does not take attention away from the main genus.

Orchids using the same or similar potting mixes as cymbidiums, *other than the sawdust mix*, makes diversification much easier when it comes to handling the plants for repotting. It does not matter very much if they are not taken in the right order but are handled as they appear to need it or as otherwise convenient.

Lycastes are not totally compatible with cymbidiums and preferably those which flower in summer to early autumn should be brought in before winter or spring flowering types. Quite a number are said to grow naturally in cool conditions or the temperature tolerance of cymbidiums, but again a reference to the climates in which growers live should be taken into account. It would be wise to exclude some lycastes in cool to cold climates.

Lycaste deppei (Loddiges-Lindley), which flowers on new growths produced in early summer, produces an abundance of flowers on the new growths in mid to late summer.

Another small, neat orchid which does the same is *Promenaea xanthina* (Lindley), with bright yellow flowers and faint perfume, which flowers at about the same time.

Sources for such orchids are the sales benches at shows or society meetings, but when buying plants there the origins should be known, particularly the altitudes at which they grow. Where possible lists of plants should be prepared for such opportunities and when making up such lists keep the rules in mind and do not crowd the main genus.

Lycaste aromatica (Graham) is variable in size but consistent in its beautiful yellow flowers and the fragrance which has something of a touch of cinnamon in it. In general the yellow to green species need a little more warmth than cool grown cymbidiums, but I grew it for years in such an association.

Preference should be shown for orchids which go through a dormant period over the colder months of the year. The life of risky plants can frequently be assured by careful watering by soaking the base of containers in shallow dishes of water rather than orthodox methods. The water should be only a couple of centimetres deep and the plants removed after a couple of minutes.

Lycaste virginalis (Scheidweiler), syn. *Lycaste skinneri* (Bateman and Lindley) has been responsible for numerous beautiful hybrids, but in cooler climates these will rely on artificial warmth over winter and spring months to retain vitality and flower satisfactorily. If they can be given winter minimum temperatures of 10 degrees Celsius (about 50 degrees Fahrenheit) with very few and short periods slightly lower, they could be included with cymbidiums.

Most lycastes have large foliage for actual pseudo-bulb size and these leaves must be protected. The plants cannot be crammed into space which does not allow the leaves to develop fully. If grown too closely the pests, notably scale, have excellent cover and may infest them before being noticed.

As a genus they grow quite well in most of the common cymbidium potting mixes, but the root system is totally different from that of cymbidiums, as outlined in the chapter on root systems.

If any special point should be emphasised it is that the better the conditions the more flowers and the longer the stems on the flowers. As the foliage is developing in its final stages and new growths show signs of thickening slightly at the base, the root systems of lycastes are usually at their most active. A careful program of fertilising with the cymbidium booster nutrient will improve the plants and flowers. The fertiliser mixture should be very weak, but at this stage, which is usually reached in late summer to winter with *Lycaste virginalis* hybrids, it is almost impossible to overwater them. The drainage should be open and free, but there is a difference between lycastes grown in plastic pots and those in clay pots. Watch this point carefully and do not mix the two.

It has often been said that the leaves of lycastes are unimportant. This is not true. All orchid foliage is important and if it deteriorates to the point where it is cast or must be removed from *Lycaste virginalis* species or hybrid plants, there is something radically wrong with the culture. The leaves should remain green right to the tips and be cast only as new growth matures and flowers are formed. With nearly all orchids there is a balance between leaf and root growth which must be sustained. There are exceptions such as calanthes, but all exceptions simply prove the rules.

Laelias are ideal additions to cymbidium collections because they may be suspended at any convenient point. They should be chosen with care and most of the Brazilian laelias avoided.

First plants added should be *Laelia anceps* (Lindley), particularly

Chamberlain's or Irvine's varieties if they can be bought or exchanged for something else, perhaps propagations of good cymbidiums. *Laelia anceps*, in company with *Laelia autumnalis* (Lindley) and *Laelia gouldiana* (Reichenbach f.), are Mexican species and will grow and flower almost down to 5 or 6 degrees Celsius (just above 40 degrees Fahrenheit). All are in the pink to mauve colour range, with some varieties having rose-purple tones. They flower in winter; the first are usually *L. anceps* varieties which start as early as May. There are also white forms.

Laelia sincorana (Schlechter), often referred to as *Laelia pumila* (Hooker) and *Laelia milleri* (Blume), are Brazilian species which grow in cool conditions. But in general the other Brazilian laelias are at risk unless grown in warmer areas of cymbidium cultivation. A good rule to follow is to avoid the yellow to gold coloured laelias, both species and hybrids.

Although some find them difficult, the small brilliant red Brazilian species sophronitis are worth inclusion. They must be treated respectfully over the summer or when they are dormant. The general tendency in orchid culture is to water heavily during summer months, but sophronitis should be watched and moistened only. If possible pots containing them should be occasionally stood in a shallow dish containing a couple of centimetres depth of water (about half an inch) with no fertiliser added. The moisture can rise up through the potting mix and maintain the plants. Free watering should only follow the appearance of fresh root growth.

It is always an achievement to produce specimen plants of these small red orchids, and a very efficient way to cultivate them is to tie them to pieces of oak or casuarina branch where the root system is obvious. They enjoy this form of cultivation and it is very easy to suspend the plants at about eye level where the root growth or dormancy can be watched. Several branch sections are suitable, but watch plant reaction carefully if treefern or cork is used.

Rossioglossum grande (Lindley) should be in any temperate zone collection. It also has a dormant period and the plants may be safely grown down among the cymbidium pots where they are unlikely to be watered until new root and plant growth are noticed. However easy for some growers, this orchid can be most intractable and difficult.

Rossioglossum grande (Lindley) and *Osmoglossum pulchellum* (Bateman and Lindley), both once known as odontoglossums, may still be bought under that name at nurseries and from some growers. *Osmoglossum pulchellum* will grow and flower in winter in temperatures of 5 to 6 degrees Celsius. Although new growths appear almost with the flowers in early to late winter, they do not

THE DENDROBIUM
This Indo-Asiatic-Australasian genus is one of the largest families of orchids in the world; it is divided into many sections and has a diverse flowering habit.

The plant depicted here, *Dendrobium* Yukidaruma 'The King', is an example of the ultimate in specialist culture. It is a derivative of the *Dendrobium nobile* complex, usually designated the softcane section of the genus.

It is seldom that plants such as this are exhibited. It was presented at the 10th Australian Orchid Conference in Adelaide, South Australia in 1986, by Bananacoast Orchids, from the central New South Wales coastal area, which is possibly the ideal climatic region for growing orchids. There is an element of chance in such a production, but it also takes skill to mature and flower it in this fashion, by following the correct fertilising and cultural system.

Few of the dendrobiums flower as consistently and well as this clone and it was perhaps an ideal choice of subject on which to exercise the art of specimen production. Unfortunately, these plants must be looked on as totally expendable, because the canes or growths, having once flowered, never do so again. A completely new plant must be grown, although if it is handled correctly and not allowed to become debilitated several new growths should emerge from the base of the flowered canes.

A strange abandonment of the hybrids derived from *D. nobile* occurred during the years preceding World War II, and the beautiful Japanese-bred rainbow of colour was never fully developed, despite its promise.

It was not a strange turn of events because the history of orchid cultivation is studded with examples of such changes in fashion, as is demonstrated by the successive editions of *Sander's List of Orchid Hybrids*.

Dendrobium (*D.* Dandy
Dame x *D.* Satan).
An unnamed grex. As fast
as the superlatives are
reached the hybridists look
into their store of possibles
and find these new
productions. This hybrid
has two unusual
dendrobiums in its
background in
D. ostrinoglossum and
D. vestigiferum, neither
of which are commonly
known.

Dendrobium (*D.* D'Bush
Classic x *D.* Gemwood).
A most unusual
development, the flower
pansy-like and very
attractive. It is a warm-
climate hybrid but appears
to be a prospective notable
addition for specialist
dendrobium growers.

Dendrobium Alleena (*D.* Helen Fukumura x *D. chrysotoxum* Lindley). This combination is unusual and resulted in a series of hybrids which inherited either the *D. bigibbum* labellum or a mid-form of the *D. chrysotoxum* pattern. The colour of the Australian species was paramount in all instances and this hybrid is referred to in the text.

THE PHALAENANTHE *Dendrobium* (*D.* Hepa x *D.* Paradise Maid), an unnamed grex. The *Dendrobium bigibbum* complex has been taken through hybridising to an ultimate specialist form like so many other genera. This flower, of about 9 centimetres, is twice the size of the original species *D. phalaenopsis* (Fitzgerald). Clones such as this are almost the ultimate material for specialists.

Dendrobium Kultana (*D.* American Beauty x *D.* Gold Flush). An example of the extraordinary colour potential in the gene pool of the phalaenanthe dendrobiums. It is a complex hybrid, with *D. schuleri*, *D. taurinum* and *D. tokai* included. When the flower is analysed relative to these dendrobiums little of them comes forward.

55

Dendrobium cuthbertsonii
(F. von Mueller). One of
the most exquisite
members of this large
genus. It grows at
considerable altitude in
Niugini, an island which
has a concentration of
orchid species not fully
known. These are
fortunately not objects of
the exploitation which
destroyed the natural flora
of so many other similarly
endowed lands, because
their habitat is protected
by impassable natural
barriers.

  D. cuthbertsonii
mostly grows in the sort
of climate not easy
to duplicate in artificial
cultivation. This plant was
grown by Geoffrey Lucas
at the Royal Botanic
Gardens, Melbourne. It grew
in a glasshouse with an
extensive collection of
bromeliads, and was never
allowed to dry out. This
treatment is consistent
with the weather pattern
of the habitat at anything
from about 1500 metres
and upward in the
extremely humid climate
of New Guinea, to use its
older and anglicised name.

  As a specialist orchid
it would need individual
day-to-day care, with the
rewards coming in the
flowers, which are about
two to two and a half
centimetres across. Colour
varies from clone to clone
and district to district
from pale cream with a
coloured labellum to the
richness of this form. It is
possible to see the habitat
mountains only rarely
because of the cloud cover,
but those fortunate
enough to have seen the
Finnisterres as Rudolf
Schlechter saw them
would agree they are
beautiful beyond
description.

BRAZILIAN LAELIA
SPECIES
(See also *Growing Orchids, Book Two.*)
Laelia sincorana (Schlechter). A cool-growing species from the state of Bahia, northern Brazil, closely resembling the single-leafed cattleyas in plant habit and flower, which is produced from the very immature new growth in early autumn. It is tolerant and appears to acclimatise to warm environments as easily as cold.

The plant habit of *Laelia sincorana* (Hooker). A newly imported plant in its first year of cultivation in cool conditions. The nature of the older part of the plant, with squat, short-leafed growths, is in contrast to the taller pseudo-bulbs and leaves developed in its new environment. It is typical of changes in morphology induced by good climatic conditions.

Laelia pumila (Hooker), Reichenbach f. The difference between the two orchids is apparent and it is surprising that both should be available with the same name. *L. pumila* is native to three states of southern Brazil, grows in a warm climate and also flowers in early to late autumn. This form has very good colour. The history of *L. pumila* is confused and contentious.

57

Laelia mantiqueirae
(Pabst). It will be apparent
that many Brazilian laelias
have been reclassified
taxonomically in the late
years of the twentieth
century, but many still
remain as originally named.
L. mantiqueirae is also
known as *L. crispilabia*
is rupicolous and with neat
habit.

Laelia perrinii (Lindley).
One of the larger, tall-
growing laelias, widespread
in central Brazilian states
and belonging to the same
group as *L. purpurata*
(Lindley). It has been
in cultivation for more
than one hundred years,
it is epiphytic and best
cultivated in containers.

Laelia itambana (Pabst). From the state of Minas Geraes, in which most of the Brazilian laelias seem to be located. The determining factor in many similar members appears to be the height to which the flower stems grow, according to Pabst and Dungs' book *Orchidaceae Brasilienses*.

Laelia kautskyi (Pabst). Native to the state of Espirito Santo in Brazil, and from a quite different climate to Minas Geraes. It is an epiphyte and would acclimatise in warm to moderate environments. A very brilliant species.

IN WARMER CLIMATES

Vandas grow best in open natural environments. As plants they can be unattractive, and the illustration of orchid root systems on page 196 makes this quite plain. It could be a matter of opinion whether any orchid plant is attractive, but again a reference to the foliage of Slippers shows how attractive they may be. Vanda flowers, while lightly brittle, have a softness of texture that frequently resembles velvet. *Vanda* (*V.* Ratana x *V.* Laurel Yap) is an unnamed grex, the unusual colour derived from the Philippines species *Euanthe* or *Vanda sanderiana* (Reichenbach f.). The reticulation or lacy pattern is also partly from the Indo-Burmese species *Vanda coerulea* (Griffith).

Vanda (*V.* Kapiolani x *V.* Opha). An unnamed grex. The colour range of the genus is rainbow-like, including blue, an unusual colour in epiphytic orchids.

60

mature until the following autumn, when *Rossioglossum grande* is almost finished flowering. Both orchids may be grown in common cymbidium mixes. The roots of *R. grande* are fairly coarse, but those of *O. pulchellum* are thinner. It may be grown into a massive plant to the stage where it overgrows itself and there is little plant deterioration. Neither should be too frequently disturbed.

If cymbidiums are grown outdoors or in a bush-house, it is unlikely that the orchids outlined above will flower with any regularity or quality. Local temperature is the principal deciding factor, as few orchids tolerate wide fluctuations, particularly in winter. Protection would be preferable, with perhaps a more sheltered spot to which they could be moved in colder months.

Some of the plants are types which could be grown over a collection of unflowering cymbidiums, but this should not be taken to extremes where flower spikes and indeed the whole plants are suffering from lack of light or other damage, say, from overwatering.

This list of hanging-type orchids which could be included in temperate-zone cymbidium collections would be incomplete without *Coelogyne cristata* (Lindley). It is most beautiful when floriferous but is probably a bitter disappointment to some when the flowers do not follow apparent good growth. It should be grown for preference in a wire basket lined with the old outer husk of elkhorn or staghorn fern or other light fibrous material.

Coelogyne cristata is inclined to be shallow rooted and must be encouraged to develop a deeper system. 'Ripening' the pseudo-bulbs with increased light at the half-way mark of their growth sometimes helps.

The potting material could be slightly modified cymbidium mix with some of the dry drainage material replaced with either oak leaf fresh fallen and chopped up, or a little peat moss. The plants should be entirely surface and if the rhizome tends to lengthen and grow out over the sides it should be forced back to the basket surface. An important part of cultivation should be never to water the plant from the top and to keep the foliage as dry as possible. The basket should be watered always from the bottom by resting it in about 5 centimetres (about 2 inches) of water and letting the moisture soak in for about five minutes. The plant should be given plenty of light, particularly as the new growths are maturing. Fertiliser should be included in the water bath in weak solution, with the residue used to fertilise any other plants that need it. One of the reasons that this orchid causes disappointment by not flowering is that its root system is too frequently short and almost surface; it should be encouraged to go to the bottom of containers.

If everything else has failed this system should be tried, giving the developing plant plenty of light to the point where the foliage may begin to look disreputable and yellowish. The signs of failure are usually browning off on leaf tips or development of black patches on the leaves. The ideal of course is nice clean mid-green foliage. The old rule of orchids growing where orchids grow applies as much to *Coelogyne cristata* as to any other in our collections.

If we go on from here to consider different genera, we begin to move into the area of forming species orchid collections. If anything could be the dream of orchid lovers it would be such a project. It is the hardest to achieve, but a great amount of flexibility is found in various genera and probably if the flowering is not all it should be the final result is worth it.

There is little enough to guide one, because most of the advocacy of this or that for such a group is written from local experience without much thought about the cosmopolitan nature of the pastime. The only real guide is experience, and that should not be at the expense of plants but rather of those who take on such collections in the first place.

The ethic, if one is to be found in orchid growing, is that a poor result after a year or two of effort would cause you to pass the plant on to another grower with better facilities, particularly if you wish to be recognised as a specialist grower.

4 PLANNING A SPECIES COLLECTION

It should not be thought that indiscriminate buying is a good way to build a species collection, but if the truth were told there are some which originated in this fashion.

Many elements of specialist collection fill-ins, such as the laelias and other orchids recommended for cymbidium collections could form the nucleus of species groups. In fact, they can frequently grow into separate groups which complement the main section. It is difficult to advise anyone how to start a species collection without first having such a base.

There is no limit to the size into which such a collection could grow and it could eventually move into a separate enclosure and diversify into suitable temperature related orchids from many genera. Some I have seen began in this way and grew into un-manageable proportions because the owners did not know when to call a halt. Plants in such collections suffer because they have been lost to sight for perhaps weeks or even months until they flower in desperation to attract attention. The largest of such collections contained 400-odd species orchids and an almost equal number of hybrid intruders in various genera.

You must discount the opinions of vendors about the hardiness or tolerance of orchids. For example, a genus which is becoming popular at any period is frequently sold as cool to cold growing when the truth might be that its recommended temperature should be a minimum of 12 degrees. Such misrepresentation is common and to look for any degree of success in the wrong set of conditions could be very costly.

Masdevallia is such a genus. The plants were known from almost the beginning of imports into Britain and Europe of orchids from South America. While some species grow at high altitudes, others are from relatively low areas which experience a great amount of warmth through the annual cycle.

In a list in front of me as I work on this there are more than one hundred species; some of the names have keys to indicate their preference for warmth or cold, but there is nothing to signify the needs of about half the list. To buy or not to buy? That is the question.

Looking for answers, if only to some of the mystery, I took Charles Schweinfurth's *Orchids of Peru* from the shelf and found that there are some forty masdevallias in Peru. I selected the first on the list, *Masdevallia amabilis* (Reichenbach f. and Warscewicz).

The collector Warscewicz found this orchid growing in Peru at an altitude of 2600 to 2800 metres (about 8500 to 9000 feet), but there was little information about the terrain and climate except that the plants grew in evergreen thickets. One would be led to believe from the altitude that it would be a cool-growing species, but the list of plants indicates that it requires warmth.

Masdevallia coccinea (Linden) also grows in Peru at about the same altitude. As those who have grown this species know, it will not acclimatise in cold conditions and requires a moderate degree of warmth. It will not excel in a cold glasshouse in a cold climate. Yet there is nothing in the list of plants to show that it requires warmth.

These are two examples of the kind of misinformation or lack of information which is a prominent feature of catalogues offering plants which are unfamiliar to prospective buyers. There is one way in which this can be moderated if not nullified and it lies in a plan to build a mixed collection for cultivation in temperatures which never fall below 12 degrees Celsius (about 53 degrees Fahrenheit) at any time of the year. A lapse of no more than 2 degrees for short periods would be a built-in safety factor. Most orchids which were supposed to be cool growing could grow and flower comfortably in such conditions.

It is worthwhile bringing masdevallias into cultivation during the bicentenary of orchid growing. Although their popularity has risen and waned over the years since introduction of *Masdevallia veitchiana* (Reichenbach f.) about 1866, following its discovery by Pearce in the Peruvian Andes at about 4500 metres (about 14,000 feet), they have never entirely lost favour. A collector named Davis who rediscovered the orchid in a similar locality but at a slightly lower altitude a few years later described its manner of growth in crevices and hollows of a rocky habitat with little or no soil. It is one of the larger masdevallias, and Veitch records the flowers as measuring 4 inches in length.

Masdevallia harryana (Reichenbach f.), which was named in honour of Harry Veitch and which some consider conspecific with *M. coccinea* (Linden), was originally regarded as highly as *M. veitchiana* (Reichenbach f.). The flowers of some of the varieties collected in those early years when the genus was first popularised were quite as large as the best of *M. veitchiana*. It is most difficult to describe the colour of either of these species because there is so much variation from one plant to another and the changing light of every new day seems to change them as well.

Some masdevallias were illustrated in *Growing Orchids, Book Three* and the history of the Veitch family is given in *Book Two*.

In *Reichenbachia*, one of the pre-eminent publications on orchids of the late years of the nineteenth century, Frederick Sander has this to say of *Masdevallia harryana*:

Our own collectors describe these masdevallias as growing in Columbia [note the spelling] near Bogota in patches—acres in extent—from 8,000 to 12,000 feet elevation, sometimes under shrubs, but often in the open in a fog-laden atmosphere, blooming in the greatest profusion in almost every conceivable shade of color—scarlet, crimson, purple and magenta being most prevalent, lighting up the whole landscape with the abundance and marvellous brilliancy of their rainbow-hued blossoms. No orchids with which we are acquainted are more easily cultivated than masdevallias, nor are there any subjects of the whole order that better repay the care bestowed upon them.

Perhaps those who have seen acres of the weed known as Patterson's Curse in flower in Australia could appreciate what those masdevallias must have looked like.

Several masdevallias flower again from stems which have already flowered. They include *M. tovarensis* (Reichenbach f.), *M. infracta* (Lindley) and *M. maculata* (Klotzsch and Karsten). Among the recommendations of the early years when they were cultivated was that the stems should not be allowed to flower a second time because the plants were weakened badly by the practice. We seem to have improved over the years, for few growers now have any qualms about letting the stems flower naturally until the plants decide that they are finished.

In the late years of the nineteenth century several growers of the genus had large collections of masdevallia species and many hybrids were raised. Some of the beautiful masdevallias are illustrated in the colour pages of this book.

Sander introduced *Masdevallia Chestertoni* (Reichenbach f.) from Colombia about 1880. It was named for one of the collectors whose history was related in *Growing Orchids, Book Three*. Unlike most of the genus it has a large labellum. It is rather rare in cultivation and eagerly sought by those who have a fancy for the genus. Its correct name is *Mas. caudata*.

Masdevallia caudata (Lindley) was one of the first of the genus to become known to European horticulturists from a dried flower received by Dr Lindley about 1830. Some of the famous names of the trade were involved in its second appearance: it was sent to William Bull, of Chelsea, by Shuttleworth with a large consignment of orchids from Colombia, at that time known as New Granada. The habitat was also described, and the fact that it was found growing with *Odontoglossum crispum* (Lindley) at an altitude of more than 6500 feet. On this occasion it grew as an epiphyte, an unusual situation for most of this genus.

A comparatively recent subdivision of the genus resulted in such genera as draculas and dryadellas being created, with some species transference to them.

Although it is possible to grow masdevallias into large plants, they are best grown in rather small pots, which may be either plastic or terracotta. As they have a liking for continuous moisture without being constantly wet, their cultivation bears a strong resemblance to odontoglossum culture. This cannot be emphasised too strongly for anyone contemplating a mixed species collection. Masdevallias will not thrive in alternating wet and dry conditions like laelias or other epiphytic orchids.

While you are learning about cultivating this genus do not be too hesitant. They are just another genus which must be treated with respect and given the same general consideration as other plants in the glasshouse.

Potting material is best kept simple. It should consist principally of two elements: bark, and either charcoal or coarse gravel with no sand in it. Small washed river pebbles about the size of a pea or a little smaller will do just as well, and if you do not object to charcoal it may also be used with the pebbles.

The bark should be sieved through a three-eighth inch mesh, which in metrics is about 1 centimetre. For the smaller plants in anything less than 70 millimetre pots (about 3 inches) this bark should be mixed with a finer grade in the proportion of two of coarse to one of fine. All dust and fine rubbish should be sieved out of both bark and charcoal, which should be of the same grade.

The proportions of the mix should be 75 per cent bark and 25 per cent charcoal or whatever. If there are only a few plants in the collection some problems may arise in keeping them moist if they are in terracotta pots. In plastic pots this mix may also seem to be a little arid and a light topping of sphagnum moss should be used on the surface.

When using terracotta pots it may be best to put the clay pot into a plastic pot which is just large enough to take it and place a small pad of sphagnum moss in the bottom of the plastic pot. The plants are watered by standing them in a shallow dish of water about 2 centimetres deep for a few minutes. It is painstaking work but there is no worry about the plants becoming too dry. The clay pot inside the plastic overcoat will stay moist for days. Between waterings the plants should be occasionally sprayed overhead in fine weather but never really soaked from above.

With experience it may become apparent that the potting mix is unsuitable and modification may be necessary. But do not change the nature of the basic materials unless you are sure of what you are doing.

Among other cool-growing orchids which should be included are the following:

Aerides vandarum (Reichenbach f.) is best fixed to a tall treefern pole planted in a potful of screenings. The roots are principally aerial but will enter the treefern and also the stone in the pot if there is anything there to attract them. Like most of these orchids they have a 'nose' for anything which offers food. Usually *A. vandarum* carries only two or three flowers but on well-grown plants as many as two or three racemes may appear together.

Vanda alpina (Lindley) is a cool-growing dwarf which also has only one or two flowers on a short raceme. It should be pot grown in coarse material to give the vandaceous roots scope for airiness. It must not be buried beneath other plants and starved for light.

Although there are arguments against suspending plants above others, and such plants may not get all the moisture they need, many of us would never get all the plants into our glasshouses and other enclosures if it were not for this part of cultivation. Maxillarias such as *M. porphyrostele* (Reichenbach f.) and *M. nigrescens* (Lindley), which may be slab grown and hung against walls, should be part of a cool-growing group. *M. nigrescens* has quite large, beautiful flowers and a sometimes overpowering scent. It flowers in late autumn and early winter, and rests through most of the really cold part of the year.

Maxillaria porphyrostele flowers in early spring and is a vigorous, easily grown orchid. It thrives on a slab of suitable material and like most of the genus appears to need little rest. Water it sparingly when there is no plant activity. It may need only infrequent watering if the environment is monitored and humidity is kept above 50 per cent.

Cattleya loddigesii (Lindley), which is sometimes labelled *C. harrisoniae* or *C. harrisoniana*, is an autumn-flowering Brazilian bifoliate cattleya which carries up to five flowers on newly made growths. These are produced in early autumn; the colour varies from white to deep mauve and the flower measures up to 10 centimetres across (about 4 inches). The pseudo-bulbs of this cattleya are slender and grow neatly close. It should be grown in usual cattleya mixes and allowed to remain dormant over winter *or until new roots are visible on new growths* or older roots. Do not water heavily until it is growing strongly then gradually increase watering and fertiliser. Odd varieties of this cattleya may not flower until spring.

Oncidium excavatum (Lindley) is a species about which there is some confusion, a cool-growing South American orchid flowering in late autumn to winter. It should be grown on a slab of bark or cork with scope for it to climb naturally toward the top of the mount. The root system is rather fine and easily destroyed if overwatered when not in active growth. Like most of the genus, the plant is accustomed to some shrivelling over its rest period; it soon picks up again as root activity and growths appear. It is summer-growing, with the flower spikes appearing in the outer leaves of new growths in the first weeks of autumn. As root activity increases and growths are about 10 centimetres high (about 4 to 5 inches), regular application of weak fertiliser will produce nice branching racemes of yellow and brown flowers two to three centimetres across. The flower stems grow rapidly up to about one metre.

There are several members of the genus sophronitis, all of them beautiful miniature gems.

Sophronitis coccinea varies considerably in plant and flower size, with the best flowers being about 7 to 8 centimetres across (about 3 inches). The colour varies slightly, but is usually rose-carmine and glistening.

Sophronitis coccinea is variable, according to Pabst and Dungs, from pale creamy yellow to yellow in the variety *rossiterana*.

Sophronitis pygmaea is usually considered to be a variety of *S. coccinea*, but where the latter flowers in late winter to spring, *S. pygmaea* flowers in late summer to early autumn. It is smaller in plant form than *S. coccinea* and has smaller flowers.

Sophronitis wittigiana (Barbosa-Rodrigues) has flowers which are coloured red-mauve, but the plant is indistinguishable from *S. coccinea* in most instances. It is frequently sold as *S. coccinea*.

Sophronitis brevipedunculata (Fowlie) is almost indistinguishable from *S. coccinea* but appears easier to grow.

These comprise the cool-growing sophronitis which would be

MASDEVALLIAS AND ODONTOGLOSSUMS

Specialising in cool-growing orchids is no easier than in tropical genera. Masdevallias prefer cooler climates because they originate at high altitudes. Unlike most epiphytes, they do not have marked dormant periods because the climates in which they grow naturally are constantly moist. This brings into focus the need in specialist cultivation for absolute control over the environments in which various genera grow. Brief periods of neglect are tolerable to many epiphytic genera but neither masdevallias nor odontoglossums, whether in their pure species form or as hybrids, will tolerate it.

There are several hundred masdevallia and closely related genera, all of which are native to Central and South American regions.

The odontoglossums exemplify the inter-relation between species and their natural hybrids. They were the subjects of close study by the earliest cultivators of the genus, not forgetting also the contribution of the collectors, who forwarded much information about the various mixtures of types and forms in the habitats. From all this material, men such as Robert Allen Rolfe traced the complex relationship between the various species and the 'in-betweens' which came to light. Unfortunately other countries, such as Australia, for example, have been ruthlessly plundered and destroyed and the original material has been lost. With it has disappeared the origin of our orchid flora and the inter-relationships between the various epiphytic orchids such as *Dendrobium kingianum* (Bidwill). The odontoglossum pictured here is a natural hybrid with an interesting history which was unravelled before the origins were lost.

Other illustrations of the genus appear on pages 135 and 136.

Masdevallia coccinea (Lindley).

Odontoglossum ruckerianum (Reichenbach f.) (A Joan Skilbeck water-colour)

Masdevallia amabilis
(Reichenbach f.). With
many other members of
the genus this orchid
could best be described as
an alpine plant. The genus
is distributed throughout
large areas of South
America, not always at
high altitudes, but
reaching its greatest
concentration on the
central branch of the
Andes in Colombia.

Several orchid collectors
of the nineteenth century
were authorities on the
genus, and it was so
liberally spread over the
continent that there was
little secrecy about the
source of the plants.
They were poor travellers,
however, and had to be
collected and dispatched at
the right time of the year
or they were total write-
offs.

Veitch, through his
agents and collectors,
amassed considerable
information about the
genus and was at pains to
point out that the moist
conditions, almost to
saturation point, in which
the plants grew were
significantly different to
the same condition of
saturation at sea level in
whatever country they
were to be artificially
grown. In the *Manual of
Orchidaceous Plants* the
scientific data is fully
outlined, but it is rather
futile for ordinary orchid
growers to attempt to
create so finely the
conditions in which to
grow masdevallias.

Mas. Amabilis (pink) with *Mas. ignea*.

If correct preliminary
design is taken seriously,
several genera combine
with a good cross-section
of the masdevallias and
one of the principal series
of orchids which can fill
the role quite well is the
odontoglossum complex.
If a good average is struck
the two genera are easy
to handle, although
masdevallias may be as
irregular in their growth
and flowering as
odontoglossums, which

may contain clones which
flower every eighteen
months, every year or
even more frequently.

It is a matter of treating
each plant individually,
increasing the fertiliser or
withholding it as necessary
when plants are inactive,
but maintaining the
humidity and rationalising
the temperature when it
exceeds the plant tolerance
in order to prevent
damaged leaves and
perhaps lost flowers.

Masdevallia veitchiana (Reichenbach f.) (top) is one of the most beautiful orchids in the world, although hard pressed for the honour by other masdevallias such as *M. coccinea* (Linden). Both grow at high altitudes and are quickly lost if temperature and humidity are wrong.

M. veitchiana was first discovered on the Andes mountains in Peru about 1867, growing 'in the crevices and hollows of the rocks with but little soil about their roots. . . . At this great altitude, notwithstanding the tenuity of the atmosphere, the heat from the direct rays of an almost vertical sun is very great on clear days, but the nights are damp and chilly. The range of temperature is therefore very considerable.'

So goes the summary offered by Veitch's *Manual of Orchidaceous Plants*. But how different a literal interpretation applied to these plants could be. All the modifying factors of environments cannot be applied to mixed collections of orchids, so we nearly always have to be satisfied with an average set of conditions suited to as many different genera as possible. But plants to accompany masdevallias should be selected with care.

How can we describe the qualifications needed to house masdevallias in particular and allow for the peculiarities of their co-residents? Well, in the first place moisture would be paramount, so we should construct a closed bench. The heat from the sun under glass is quite different from the sun's heat at high altitudes where water vapour is always present. The ups and downs of temperature for most of the year could be partly disregarded provided the variation was within limits. All that, difficult as it may be to design, could give a fair chance of seeing flowers and growth in its season.

71

Masdevallia elephanticeps
(Reichenbach f.).
Originally found growing
on the mountains at an
altitude of 2000 to 3000
metres (about 6500 to
10,000 feet) between
Ocana and Pamplona,
Colombia. The name
originated from the
fancied resemblance to an
elephant's head and trunk
when viewed from a
certain angle.

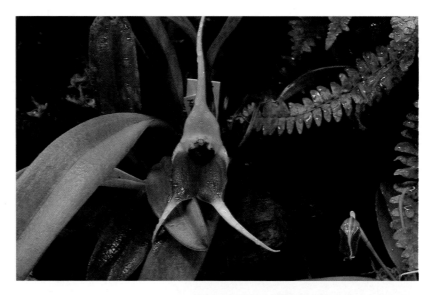

Masdevallia Kimballiana
(*M. caudata* Lindley x *M.
veitchiana* Reichenbach
f.). An early hybrid, raised
by Sander in the
1890–1900 period and a
moderately sized, beautiful
flower. In 1945 only about
fifty hybrid masdevallias
had been raised and
named. The genus went
out of fashion about 1900.

Masdevallia Doris
(*M. racemosa* Lindley x
M. triangularis Lindley).
A smaller hybrid but
developed from a strange
pair because *M. racemosa*
is morphologically unlike
most of the genus with its
long raceme of flowers
from a creeping rhizome.
M. Doris conforms to the
normally accepted plant
structure.

Miltoniopsis warscewiczii
(Reichenbach f.), a
member of a genus more
common in Colombia than
other states of South
America. They are the
progenitors of a hybrid
complex of pansy-like
flowers which dislike
temperature variations
below about 15 degrees.
The hybrids are difficult
to manage except as
specialist collections and
even then take a lot of
understanding.

Miltoniopsis Mary Stewart.
Some conception of the
mass of flower which may
be developed on these
plants under good
cultivation is indicated by
this specimen. Any
grower, having once
flowered a plant such as
this, is more apt to become
a specialist than those who
toy with the genus by
growing odd specimens.

THE BRAZILIAN SOPHRONITIS

A genus about which there is confusion. A reference to *Orchidaceae Brasilienses*, by Pabst and Dungs, one of the most modern texts and well illustrated, will disclose differences compared with other texts.

Sophronitis brevipedunculata (Cogniaux) occurs in the state of Minas Geraes in Brazil, mostly growing on rocks but also epiphytically. It is morphologically indistinguishable from *S. coccinea* and there is also a strong resemblance to that orchid in the flowers.

Sophronitis pygmaea is a
sub-species of *S. coccinea*
(Lindley). It is diminutive,
with pseudo-bulbs about 2
centimetres long and the
leaves also that length. It
grows and flowers freely
in a moderate climate and
not quite as well in
cool conditions. Unlike
S. coccinea, it flowers in
middle to late summer.

THE SPECIMEN PLANT
Lycaste Shoalhaven

Most genera are capable of producing sufficient flowers to make them an attractive prospect for growing into what are usually referred to in orchid growing as specimen plants. These plants resemble in a large degree those plants originally imported from their habitats in the earlier days of orchid culture.

There are two ways in which such plants may be grown. The first is by cheating a little and planting two or more propagations of the same clone in one container and it is when flowered a somewhat spurious claim to have grown this production into specimen status.

The second way is a greater test of the skill. It consists of beginning with either a small propagation or a section of a clone which has the necessary qualifications for the proposition and growing it progressively until it reaches the maximum potential to be realised from the plant and the facilities.

This lycaste was grown in the latter way. It was a normal small propagation selected because the clone was capable of producing six or more flowers from one pseudo-bulb. In the photograph on page 150 it is photographed in its early stages as a doubling of the growth in one year.

The two pseudo-bulbs matured and each produced seven flowers. Within the real meaning of the term specimen plant it may not qualify, but with fourteen large flowers, each of which was about 12 centimetres across (about 5 inches) it represented an achievement.

Some genera are not particularly good subjects for this form of culture, but it should be an ambition in every grower to achieve some notable exhibits. In a long life of orchid growing the author has produced several, among them this lycaste. Each was a wonderfully satisfying end to a long-term project.

possible in cymbidium company as hanging plants rather than benched. Nomenclature and identification of the genus is confusing and irregular.

Sophronitis cernua is best left to warmer climates and even so is rather touchy for many growers.

When these small orchids are mounted on branch sections, cork, or bark mounts they should have a small pad of moss inserted under the base of the plants. If they are grown on treefern, which is occasionally used, they should be tied on bare, as the treefern is absorbent and carries moisture to sustain plants between waterings.

All the sophronitis are essentially open-root epiphytes, most of them growing naturally on rock faces and ledges as well as trees. They are extremely durable plants. The root systems of most of the sophronitis are neither vigorous nor profuse in artificial cultivation, but when they are grown open-rooted they can be watched for growth tips and the plants encouraged to either grow or remain dormant as the case may be. Whenever a slab of treefern, cork or any other type appears to be unsuitable, do not hesitate to discard it.

Overwatering is the principal reason why growers fail with sophronitis. The natural humid environment of a well-adjusted glasshouse can maintain them for quite a long time, and the temptation to water because they appear to be dry should be resisted.

Australian sarcochilus prefer shade and will grow in the leafy situation under cymbidiums, although they would need to be closely watched for scale and other pests in this situation. This genus is no more susceptible than most orchids, but pests thrive in hiding places where there is less surveillance.

Most of the sarcochilus will grow on slabs of bark, treefern or cork, whereas *S. hartmannii* (F. Mueller) does better when potted in ordinary cymbidium mix. A successful method is to cut broad slits in the sides of plastic pots and line them with staghorn or elkhorn leaf or similar organic waste, before filling them and planting the sarcochilus growths.

S. falcatus (Robert Brown) is a very easy orchid to grow, as is *S. olivaceous* (Lindley). *S. ceciliae* (F. Mueller) needs a bit more care because it seems to prefer growing on stone of some sort. A potful of screenings or other rock should prove a good base with a little moss topping added to hold moisture. Its natural habitat situation is on rock and it is sometimes hard to break such orchids out of their preferences.

Most of the species will grow on slabs of bark, cork or treefern, although the lastnamed material has often been found unsuitable.

If grown in a glasshouse they should be tried in the shadiest places, and their origins suggest *a constant state of dampness for much of the year.* If you watch the roots of these open-grown orchids in the cooler months, you will find that they frequently seal off the tips. In such conditions the plants need only a slight swish over with the hose once a week to keep them in good condition.

When flowering, the stems are vulnerable to pests, particularly slugs and snails. Earwigs also find them attractive. When the stems appear, the plants should be kept damp but not wet until the roots show activity, particularly *S. hartmannii.*

Although this section is principally concerned with formation of groups wholly of species or a combination of species and hybrid orchids of different genera, some thought could be given at this point to converting one of these subsidiary genera into a main section of the collection. It frequently happens.

One reason for combining other orchids with specialist genera is to have flowers in the seasons when the main collection is out of flower, but this can be easily lost sight of when the buying splurge begins. It is impossible to satisfy the need for flowers in the off-season entirely because there are insufficient orchids to do this. The principal flowering season for most is spring and there is no reason to bypass a worthwhile genus like pleione for a cool-climate collection because it flowers in the flush season. Cymbidiums and other cool-flowering things like odontoglossums are the only genera with which pleiones are completely compatible.

It is possible to restrict a total collection to pleiones and have other compatible genera as the fill-ins, but if your pleiones are only subsidiary to cymbidiums it is best to buy the cheapest and simplest forms of the genus. The commonest is probably *Pleione formosana* (Hay), which is reasonably easy to grow and goes into a fairly long dormancy once the flowers are gone and the growths are mature.

Pleiones are best grown in shallow dishes rather than pots and they may thrive in most cymbidium potting mixes with a little crumbled sphagnum moss added to keep the material moist.

Some growers dry out the saucers, dishes or pans thoroughly once the foliage falls from the corms or pseudo-bulbs, but this is not always necessary. Nor is it necessary to repot the plants every year when they are grown as fill-ins. But it is wise to dry them off slightly when they are dormant. If repotting becomes necessary it should be done as soon as the new shoots appear at the base of the old bulbs.

Some pleiones also have the habit of producing tiny corms on the tops of pseudo-bulbs. Initially they look like tendrils such as appear on sweet peas, but if planted they develop into tiny additions to the collection.

Most orchids considered in the previous paragraphs could well be converted into sections of species collections with fairly wide scope, and they are by no means the total catalogue of genera which would acclimatise and grow adjacent to cymbidiums. But the real meaning of the term cool should be kept in mind when considering additions. *There may be a bit of flexibility for cool orchids to adapt to temperate or slightly warmer conditions, but there is little scope for temperate or warmer growing subjects to adapt to cool or cold.*

Catalogues and sales sheets from orchid nurseries are printed for all classes of growers. But the specialist should look at them with critical eyes, particularly if they include colour illustrations. Each genus has its pitfalls and a few questions about the contents of catalogues would be appropriate: Do the plants fit into warm, cool or intermediate collections? Are they moist growers or hardy types which are tolerant? Will they acclimatise in the conditions which you can offer? It may be found that the advertiser of the wares has formed classifications to fit the climate in which he lives.

Having considered genera which prefer moist conditions, it would be appropriate to turn to the epiphytes which need fairly dry dormant periods: these include catasetums and their associates and many oncidiums. Dry or arid does not mean total deprivation of moisture as some people appear to imagine. These terms indicate that plants are easily damaged by application of moisture to the wrong parts at the wrong time in their annual cycle. The root systems are vulnerable and may be protected only by keeping them dry or nearly so. *The humidity or atmospheric moisture in enclosures has nothing to do with dryness or aridity of plants because it should be one of the constants.*

As experience and the exchange of knowledge between growers indicate, there are many hundreds of species and hybrids which fit well into collections, depending on natural climates. Although each grower buys speculatively at times, one must be sure that plants are reasonably suited rather than risk losses, particularly where species orchids are concerned.

Make sure that your plants are clearly labelled. The name may be out of date, but that is fairly general in orchid growing. Plants may be labelled in the form 'Something x Something'. Try to find the name of the cross-pollination in *Sander's List of Orchid Hybrids*. It may not have been registered, but at the earliest opportunity the correct name should be put on the plant or plants. *Sander's List* has been updated every five years to 1980 at the beginning and in the middle of each decade.

It is common for orchid growers to concentrate on different genera as time goes by. Most abandon a chosen genus for various specific reasons, not least of which is that they made a poor initial choice. A new start is better than a totally mediocre orchid-growing career.

The selection of periodic dry-growing genera or species for either species and hybrid collections, or as combination plants to grow with main genera, should be made with the same care and attention to temperature ranges as the selection of moist-growing orchids.

5 CATTLEYAS

The word cattleya scarcely does justice to the conglomerate group which comprises plants as widely known and grown as any other orchids. All hybrids are referred to generally as cattleyas, whether they are laeliocattleyas or any other combination.

Irrespective of any external climates they will produce the same quality flowers in protected enclosures, provided temperature, light and moisture are given proper attention.

The maximum advisable temperature ranges for this group are summer 30 to 34 degrees Celsius (about 85 to 95 degrees Fahrenheit) and winter or cool season minimum of 13 to 15 degrees Celsius (about 55 to 60 degrees F.). Minor aberrations from these temperatures are unimportant.

It is best to consider first all the combinations of species and genera involved, beginning with cattleya as a genus. The hybrids within the genus are commonly divided between single-leafed cattleyas and bifoliates, with the *Cattleya labiata* (Lindley) section holding pre-eminence. The original plant of the species was discovered in Brazil, and some authorities hold this as the basis for the larger single-leafed cattleya species as a whole.

The so-called varieties of *C. labiata* are considered as separate species in the context of such a summary as this, both because they are designated so in *Sander's List of Orchid Hybrids* and because they originated in widely separated habitats of the various South American states.

The bifoliate cattleyas are best regarded as separate again, because they represent a completely different type of flower from the *C. labiata* section. They are, however, compatible with that section and most of the other genera with which it is involved.

The principal members of the *Cattleya labiata* section are: *C. dowiana* (Bateman and Reichenbach), of which *C. dowiana* var.

Brassolaeliocattleya
Memoria Helen Brown
The specialist cattleya
grower in the bicentenary
years moved away slightly
from the orthodoxy of the
1930 to 1980 period to
give more importance to
the colour factors in these
flowers, with emphasis on
contrast—greens with red
labellums, whites with
brilliant purple-red
labellums and yellows to
gold with blush tints in
the labellum instead of
solid colour. This
brassolaeliocattleya has a
green breeding line behind
it. (A Geoffrey Skilbeck
ink drawing)

aurea is the outstanding flower; *C. eldorado* (Lindley and Veitch), *C. gaskelliana* (Sander), *C. mendelii* (Backhouse), *C. mossiae* (Hooker), *C. percivaliana* (Reichenbach f.), *C. rex* (O'Brien), *C. trianaei* (Lindley and Reichenbach), *C. schroderae* (Reichenbach), which some consider to be a variety of *C. trianaei*, *C. warneri* (T. Moore), *C. warscewiczii* (Reichenbach f.), also known as *C. gigas*; and *C. lawrenceana* (Reichenbach f.). *Cattleya lueddemanniana* (Reichenbach f.), a Venezuelan member of the *C. labiata* section, is rarely noted in cultivation.

The bifoliate section, that is, those which produce two short, rounded or spear-blade leaves on rather thin, elongated pseudobulbs, could be considered as centred on *Cattleya loddigesii* (Lindley) or *C. intermedia* (Graham).

Other members are *C. brownii* (Rolfe), *C. elatior* (Lindley), *C. forbesii* (Lindley), *C. violacea* (Humboldt, Bonpland, Kunth), *C. acklandiae* (Lindley), *C. bicolor* (Lindley), *C. velutina* (Reichenbach f.), *C. granulosa* (Lindley), *C. porphyroglossa* (Lindley and Reichenbach f.), *C. amethystoglossa* (Linden and Reichenbach f.), *C. guttata*

(Lindley) and *C. schilleriana* (Reichenbach f.). Some of these are frequently regarded as varieties of other species and many have not been included in this short list. The most important are included.

In alliance with laelias, rhyncolaelias (referred to as brassavolas for the purposes of *Sander's List of Orchid Hybrids*), sophronitis, diacrium, broughtonia, epidendrum, schomburgkia, domingoa, cattleyopsis and other genera, the complex is huge and not all held under the total heading of cattleya. Some are known as potinaras yet are still referred to casually as cattleyas.

The complex, however, is in general sub-tropical and tropical, with a minor portion, notably in the bifoliate species and hybrid section, suited to moderate temperate climates. Some members, one of which is illustrated in *Growing Orchids, Book Two*, are cold tolerant.

The specialist who grows cattleyas should purchase good species as well as hybrids. Only first-class clones are worth the trouble in this phase of the pastime. This should not be taken to advocate discard and destruction, but poorer forms should be replaced with better as opportunities come along. When buying from mericlone lists, remember the disabilities of the system and do not rely on printed colours or glowing descriptions in catalogues.

In returning to 1894 and a summary of the species *Cattleya trianaei* in the *Orchid Review*, the editor Rolfe brought to light more than fifty well-known varieties of this cattleya, all of which had merit over and above general species level. Some of them are illustrated in *Growing Orchids, Book Two*.

If any rules could be laid down for growing these quality species cattleyas they would include buying for duplication or even triplication of clones derived from meristem tissue. That duplication is a necessity is shown by the comparative photographs of the mericlones of *Brassolaeliocattleya* Malworth 'Orchidglade'.

For a number of reasons, not least of which is the conglomerate background, cattleyas seem prone to vary when propagated as mericlones. Under normal vegetative propagation there is little or no change, no matter how many plants are developed from original clones. The reason for doubling or perhaps trebling an order for a mericlone propagation of any cultivar is that it provides material from which to select the best and dispose of the remainder. It may be that each clone is first class, but a little different. The whole process becomes very complicated at this point, where a completely new variety may be born out of the original. It has occurred in cymbidiums so is not impossible in cattleyas. The whole of the varietal naming process is called into question.

Any approach to specialist growing of cattleyas should be based on climate and its control. Within reason there are no restrictive climates. For example, where the coastal region of eastern Australia about 35 degrees south latitude is the ideal outdoor climate for cymbidium culture, the coastal region of about 25 to 30 degrees south latitude provides ideal weather patterns for cattleya culture with minimum protection.

The reality, of course, is that in both situations some climatic and flowering protection is necessary. The cattleya complex thrives best in the *constant temperature range* of about 13 to 27 degrees Celsius (about 55 to 80 degrees Fahrenheit) and in a climate which is lightly humid. Natural humidity usually increases as the temperature drops, but in climates where high humidity is matched by high temperatures of about 30 to 35 degrees (about 85 to 95 degrees Fahrenheit) cattleya plants may be at risk and should be dried off by any possible means.

Most of the risk is from fungus spores developing and multiplying rapidly, particularly on the softer parts of plants such as new growth, flowering sheaths or buds or any cavity natural to the plants. Where photosynthesis is at a high rate, such as in new growth, these parts of plants become overloaded with moisture, spores develop and grow, and the soft tissue of the plants quickly rots as the fungus invades it.

All the technical detail about this is available if required, but so far as growers are concerned, prevention is more important than understanding the details of the disaster.

Most prevention is based on the principle of extracting heat and moisture from the plants. In climates where it is commonly hot with high humidity all design and construction must be aimed at creating the greatest possible air flow about the plants to take unwanted moisture away, thus cooling them at the same time. A contrast occurs in cooler climates, where the highest humidity in structures occurs when the temperature drops. In either instance the design should incorporate fans, if only to give additional air flow. In cooler climates it may be necessary only to move the air about inside the structure, rather than to exhaust it through ventilators.

You would expect that hotter climates would favour specialist cattleya cultivation, but the opposite is frequently true. Temperate climates have much to offer in planning a more or less natural environment for cattleyas. But there is no real reason why the complex should prove troublesome at all if the planning is right.

It is a help in growing them if individual seasons of plants are known. Some flower from newly matured pseudo-bulbs, some flower from sheaths developed in autumn and held until spring,

Cattleyas have been known by European races for some two hundred years, first in their pure form as a genus and from about half-way in their period of cultivation in hybrid form within the genus and through several generic cross-pollinations. They were also known and grown by the populations of the countries of origin for perhaps many centuries before their exploitation after contact with European races.

The story of the first of the *Cattleya labiata* series has been related in *Growing Orchids, Book Two*, and a flowering plant of this first introduction is beautifully illustrated in Frederick Sander's *Reichenbachia*, one of the delightful pieces of literature associated with the cult produced in its middle—and some would say best—years.

Cattleyas in their various appearances are probably the most generally cultivated orchids because they adapt to so many cultural patterns and climatic conditions. Environments can be created for them without the detail and expense associated with more demanding tropical conglomerates or plants such as cymbidiums, which fit poorly into warmer cultural environments.

There are many wonderful tales about the finding and bringing into cultivation of the genera now enjoyed by orchid growers of the world, but in general their collection and trans-shipment was hard, dirty and dangerous work and the glamorised tales had little foundation in fact.

The cattleya of the bicentenary years of orchid culture bears little resemblance to the species from which it has been drawn. It has in its flowers up to three or four genera through cross-pollination and hybridising. All this miscegenation has produced beauty beyond that of the original species because the people involved sought to combine all the characters they wanted from each genus involved.

Cattleya labiata (Lindley). In comparing photographs of this cattleya with lithographs it is obvious that artists, as ever, allowed themselves a bit of licence in their portrayals. This flower is on a very old plant, a propagation about the history of which there is no doubt, dating from the year 1909.

Cattleya percivaliana (Reichenbach f.). With the other cattleya on this page, different forms of which were used to create the bicentenary period cattleyas and intergeneric hybrids, it belongs to a group of orchids unsurpassed by other genera for colour and beautiful symmetry. A number of other affiliates to the group are noted in the text.

*Brassavola (rhyncolaelia)
digbyana* (Lindley), a
Central American species
with warm-growing
characteristics. (Top)

Laelia purpurata (Lindley
and Paxton), a Brazilian
species with warm-
growing characteristics.
(Centre.)

The three genera in total
are the background to the
primary hybrid cattleyas,
laeliocattleyas and
brassocattleyas, also the
secondary hybrid
brassolaeliocattleyas.
Laeliocattleyas far
outnumber any of the
other categories and
possibly outnumber the
total of all the others.

The smaller cattleya
species, particularly the
bifoliate section, have
their counterparts to the
larger and perhaps better
known *labiata* section.

The other members
concerned in the
development of the
cattleya complex
embodying *labiata* or two-
leafed species are detailed
in the text.

Cattleya mossiae (Hooker)
Lindley, a Venezuelan
species with warm-
growing characteristics.
(Bottom.)

Cattleya trianaei (Linden and Reichenbach) was originally found in New Granada (Colombia) about 1842 so far as the records relate and it was Linden who received the credit. While it may be wrong to select any one of the so-called *C. labiata* series as pre-eminent, Linden's discovery brought an amazing wealth of colour and variety to the cultivators of the time. The history of the species is recorded in the *Orchid Review* and from this account it would appear that it was known and grown first in England in the collection of Rucker about 1848.

C. trianaei grew naturally over a fairly wide area of Colombia and was noted for the magnificent flowering of masses of the plants before being overcollected and almost totally destroyed. Its name was a matter of disagreement and it will be noted that it is differently spelled in *Growing Orchids, Book Two*, with the final vowel omitted.

It is possible to trace a number of varieties of *C. trianaei* which could be included with distinction in any specialist orchid collection. This project, which would take some time to carry out, would be a notable achievement for any orchid grower.

The flowering season of *C. trianaei* is usually early spring, although it varies according to environment and the natural climate in

which it is grown. The colour varies from a pure white form with an orange-yellow or pale yellow patch on the central portion of the labellum, to fairly deep rose-pink forms with deeper colouring on the labellum.

For the information of interested growers, more than sixty varieties of merit were recorded in 1895, any one of which had quality equal to the most prized hybrid cattleyas of the bicentenary years of the cult.

Cattleya trianaei (Linden and Reichenbach f.). Compared with the illustration of this cattleya on the opposite page, which according to the graph in *Growing Orchids, Book Two* would fall into the lower section or 'C' line, this flower is slightly better formed and would conform to the type of flower denoted 'B'.

Cattleya trianaei (Linden and Reichenbach f.). A sibling from the cross-pollination of a 'C' line clone and an 'A' line form of the species, which would naturally tend to bring the resultant grex principally into the 'B' section of the graph, the natural cross-flow which could be expected to stabilise the species in its natural environment.

Cattleyas for specialist growing should be selected by seeing flowering plants rather than by relying on photographs, because only the best flowers are chosen for illustration. The test of any first class cattleya is lasting quality. The three illustrated here had all been open for about ten days when photographed.

Cattleya Tiffin Bells (*C.* White Blossom x *C.* Bow Bells) was bred from albino forms of the species to follow a line of pure colour with a yellow-throated labellum. An antecedent was *Cattleya* Edithiae, an old but notable secondary hybrid.

Growing systems: Most cattleyas are grown in pots and the method illustrated here gives the best system. It takes no more room than benching; the plants have a good air circulation, and they are more easily watched. In such cultivation they should be suspended at about hip height. They are easily moved to take advantage of shading or to protect the flowers. The overhead points must be strongly supported.

BRASSOCATTLEYAS
Brassocattleya Laurel Kerr (*Bc* Deesse x *Cattleya* Jose Marti). The relatively long pedigree of this hybrid has carried the heritage of the rhyncolaelia labellum. The overall colour of the flower is in keeping with the usual trend in brassavola breeding lines.

Brassocattleya Mount Hood (*Bc* Deesse x *C.* Claris). There are fewer brassocattleyas than other inter-generic hybrids and the limiting factor is perhaps best expressed as having something to do with shape of flowers, because the ultimate of the search looked more like fulfilment by persisting with laelia breeding lines. The colour of *Bc* Mount Hood is most delicate.

LAELIOCATTLEYAS

There is more scope for colour when using laelias for inter-generic cross-pollinations. *Laelia purpurata* (Lindley-Paxton) and *Laelia tenebrosa* (Rolfe) both contribute size, and the last named has the copper colour inherited by this flower. There is also a link between the flowers in the immediate parents. In choosing specialist clones in this section of the complex it would be possible to fill an enclosure of some 20 metres by 5 metres, every plant in which would be top class, even though some of them could be as much as fifty years old.

Top: *Laeliocattleya* Jourtip (*Lc* Lisa Ann x *Lc* Copperglen).

Bottom: *Laeliocattleya* Pirate King 'Port Wine' (*Lc* Lee Langford x *Lc* Quadroon).

92

some flower from the apex of pseudo-bulbs without developing sheaths and in unusual instances from half-made pseudo-bulbs. Many of the latter are hybrids with a background inherited from *Laelia pumila* (Hooker) or *Laelia sincorana* (Schlechter). Frequently these two are considered conspecific. They are quite dissimilar, cool-growing, morphologically cattleya-like and produce the flowers from half-made pseudo-bulbs in early to late autumn. They seem out of place in the section to which they are assigned.

The other principal member of the inter-breeding program is *Laelia purpurata* (Lindley and Paxton), also a Brazilian species, but a complete contrast in all essential details to the other two.

Growers often inscribe data on the labels inserted in pots, but it is far better to enter the details of each plant in a small notebook. Do not trust to memory, because complete information about the plants in even a modest collection is too difficult to remember from year to year or even for a few weeks.

Perfection in cattleya growing depends on good potting material. Root systems should show no signs of tip failure on contact with potting material and if this does occur the material should be discarded for use with another genus and a new lot bought in. If only one plant is affected, other things may be to blame.

Each country has its own sources for bark, and there is little doubt that some is better than others. When osmunda fibre was used, some consignments were very poor indeed and root systems were affected.

If additives are used, such as charcoal, it is probably more at fault than the bark. But cheap, poor-quality bark is seldom of much use, however much it is weathered before use.

American fir bark appeared to be superior in some ways to ordinary pine bark. The pH value or relative acidity appeared to be more to the liking of cattleyas, and fir bark also appeared to retain moisture better. If this factor is present in a minor degree it is all to the good. It may be worth getting an acidity test if you are in doubt, and the ideal reading is slightly acid.

Like other orchids, cattleyas require a program of fertilising through their growing and flowering periods. The potting material efficiency will be altered if such a program calls for heavy fertiliser application and consequent flooding to leach or flush it out again. If leaf colour is pallid and the plants somewhat lifeless, a very light top-dressing of lime watered through the bark is often a good corrective. A change in fertilising method would appear necessary if the plants are like this.

Next in importance are enclosures, starting with orientation. In the southern hemisphere north-facing skillion-roofed designs give

There is little accommodation on most house allotments for a series of glasshouses such as that illustrated in the introduction. Nevertheless, some commercial establishments are much larger than this and at times contain thousands of plants in all stages of growth and size.

These two designs are suited to different genera but each could be adapted to any genus. Both are designed to be placed east–west; with the long side facing north for certain genera, and south for such things as paphiopedilums, odontoglossums, masdevallias and other genera requiring less light.

The skillion-roof design is ideal for cattleyas or dendrobiums grown in temperate to mildly sub-tropical climates, preferably with the plants hanging from independent support and clear of the ground, at anything from knee high to hip high. If benches are used for these genera, the pathways should be planned so that no plant is more than arm's length from the edge of the bench.

The ventilators at the bottom should be positioned where they will get the best draught, and should be covered with flywire. The upper ventilators should provide one vent for every two metres of length of the ridge. In the skillion-roof design no ventilators are

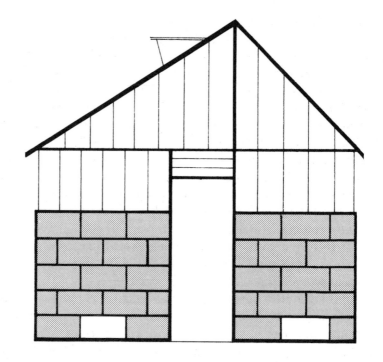

shown, but the same proportion of ventilated space should be allowed, with the ventilators hinged to the upper member of the roofing.

These designs are not made in commercial form and must be built,

although most makers of prefabricated units have a skillion-roof design.

An east–west plan for the northern hemisphere would be directly opposite that outlined above.

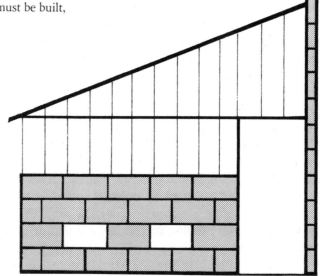

the best possible aspect. Species and hybrids alike will tolerate bright light, providing they are never exposed to direct sunlight. For the tropics it may be necessary to change this design, but for temperate to lower sub-tropical climates it can be recommended. Two designs are illustrated. For cattleyas the skillion-roofed design is better with a brick wall on the south side for warmth storage. Other designs, such as double walls filled with insulating batts, can be built with fibro-cement sheeting and are equally effective. Any timber used should be treated pine or similar wood. Design of such glasshouses is illustrated in *Growing Orchids, Book One*.

Prefabricated glasshouses with aluminium members are the easiest to build. Everything is predrilled, and although the job is easier with two people it can be done by one. It is doubtful if prefabricated structures cost more than custom-built ones where the major cost is for labour to erect the structure.

There are some deficiencies in prefabricated aluminium glasshouses which are most difficult to overcome. For example, fitting a plastic sheet liner to insulate the building against drastic loss of heat is probably the most exasperating part of orchid growing as a whole. This internal liner is necessary in cold climates, particularly for the warm-growing orchids.

In warm climates, as one would expect, the cattleya complex takes the place of cymbidiums as a specialist group of orchids. The structures for growing them are quite different from those required further south. Openness is essential for airiness, and overhead roofing should protect the plants where possible. Some idea of these structures is given in the various illustrations. Growers in northern Australia are no better positioned to grow cattleyas than those living in southern states of the continent. They also have their problems. The advantages of natural climates cannot be denied, but if thorough planning and work toward a specialist proposition is carried through the worst features of most climates can be brought to negative effect.

THE BUYING AND GROWING PLAN

There is little reason to imagine that there are differences in quality between the flowers of cattleyas, laeliocattleyas, brassocattleyas or brassolaeliocattleyas, which are referred to as cattleyas. Quality depends to a large extent on prepollination research and planning by hybridists and this, of course, figures among the imponderables of the cult. At times the quality of parents has little significance if results are analysed on the basis of subsequent flowers.

Differences should be apparent in labellum shapes and patterns when *Brassavola (Rhyncolaelia) digbyana* (Lindley) has been used in cross-pollinations. Indeed, if some of the flowers are studied relative to the names of the parents involved it is quite obvious that they are not at all what they are claimed to be. That, however, is one of the unfortunate characteristics of the orchid world as a whole, despite the extensive and well-kept catalogue of names.

It is good planning for purchasers of quality cattleyas or intergeneric hybrids to have some idea of the size of flowers expected from the plants they buy. Occasionally this is part of descriptions but more frequently not. Perhaps the background breeding will give indications. For example, if an attractive flower has a small laelia or sophronitis in the pedigree there is some likelihood that it will be only moderately sized.

This is not a real consideration when thinking along the lines of colour such as *Sophrolaeliocattleya* Anzac or *Slc* Jewel Box and other things bought for their brilliance. However, you will be very disappointed if you are expecting something of the order of 140 to 150 millimetres (about 5 to 6 inches) when the background breeding indicates something about half that size.

The specialist should try to learn all there is to know about the genera embodied in that rather loose term cattleya. Much information is contained in literature associated with the pastime, but a lot of it is expensive. The magazines and periodicals issued throughout the orchid-growing communities are cheaper and contain a wealth of information. It may not all be relevant to the country in which growers live, but a cross-reference is always helpful.

Quality Stream 'Cattleyas': The 800 Collection, published by the Japan Orchid Growers' Association, clearly indicates the course a specialist grower of cattleyas should be taking. It illustrates the best hybrids and species superbly in fairly accurate colour. It also uses the word cattleya in the same sense as this book.

Assembling a collection of cattleyas takes some time, but unlike cymbidium or paphiopedilum hybrids these flowers will never age. Once a good cattleya, always a good cattleya. And if specialising is your aim it is far better to start off slowly, and work toward such a goal without too much deviation into an exotic miscellany—a bad habit with all orchid growers.

There is some justification for asking whether it is economic or wise buying propagations or seedlings from another country when so much material is available in almost every country where orchids are commonly grown. While I do not wish to disparage orchid plants or their producers anywhere in the world, there may be radical differences between seedlings raised from original clones and those raised from pollinations of mericlones of those orchids. The mericlones may be as far away as second or third generation from original clones and some appraisal of this appears in the various colour illustrations.

Cattleyas and similar genera are true epiphytes and should not be grown in pots as we cultivate them. Their whole existence is based on exposed root systems, although parts of these systems are buried under mosses, lichens and other growth in nature. The plants have become environmentally accustomed to that, possibly because of the food gain from it. We subvert them and grow them in containers for convenience.

Ordinarily in cultivation cattleya plants are benched, but over many years seekers after quality have suspended their potted cattleyas from a reinforced and well-propped roof or from special frames built to take the weight. This is illustrated in the colour section on cattleyas on page 90.

Benches should be hip high, and suspended plants should preferably be at the same level where they can all be seen. Aeration in the hanging method is much better and moisture constantly rising from the floor encourages roots to go to the bottom of pots or leave them entirely through the aeration holes. No growth other than mosses and low ferns should be allowed to grow below the plants and none at all in the pots. Some of the best flowering cattleya collections are grown in this way.

There are advantages and disadvantages in suspending the plants, but if only as protection from pests which eat roots, shoots and flowers it is worth considering. Although it restricts the number of plants accommodated, remember that specialising is quite different from the numbers game.

The type of pots used, plastic or clay, is immaterial and they may be suspended more closely than those benched. Roots are inclined to stray a little from pot to pot, but no more than with benched plants and they have more encouragement to become naturally aerial.

Where cattleyas are grown benched, an open mesh top should be used so that there is air flow about the plants. These tops should not be so wide that it is difficult to reach the plants at the further side. Expensive plants need constant watching to ensure that the growths do not decay, that the buds are protected, and that the plants are properly spaced to give good presentation.

It should be possible to have top-quality flowering of every clone each year if common-sense propagation plans are followed. Starting with only one plant is a handicap. As soon as possible duplicates of each clone should be created by severing the older and flowered pseudo-bulbs from the newer sections of the plants. This should be done by following the rule to leave at least three older growths behind the leading or new growth in the year before repotting so that a propagation is also ready at that time.

New root growth or new tips on older roots should be the guide for growing the collection. The decision to repot, or simply to make divisions in the rhizome, must be made for each individual plant. The complete collection should not be handled in any one year. Sometimes either process may mean sacrificing flowers or limiting the time they are left on plants. They should be removed before opening if necessary.

While plants with buds moving in sheaths, and also those which have apparent buds without sheaths, should be left until the flowers are gone, it is possible to process them in minor ways such as making divisions without much harm. If possible lessen the number of flowers so that there is no real drain on vitality. Do not cut the flowers too soon or they will quickly wilt. The usual sign that they are mature is release of perfume, however faint.

Reference to the photographs should indicate the sort of root activity to look for. It is common to all epiphytic orchids and need not necessarily refer only to the genus photographed.

Poor plants, those recently imported and quarantined, and those repotted in the previous handling season will probably have disappointing flowers. Unlike cymbidiums, most epiphytes take their time in re-establishing. A better result should be obtained in twelve months' time and this system of planning and working toward the next season should be a guiding principle in all specialist culture. Each plant could be considered individually and some sort of plan worked out for it—when to sever older parts of the plant, perhaps whether to move it to another position in the glasshouse or enclosure, and when it should be supplied with nutrient.

Severed portions of plants have a much better chance of retaining foliage if they are cut before deteriorating too far. If the foliage falls off immediately the cuts are made, it is fairly certain that the severed portion has no live root and has been subsisting on the newer growths. It may propagate or it may not. Sometimes these dead-looking leafless pieces will produce shoots if they are put into plastic bags with a scrap or two of moss, the neck of the bag tied and then hung where they get fairly good light.

When following planned propagation it is possible to have plants of each good variety flowering every year. After paying high prices for hybrid cattleyas or species, a planned growing program should allow return of some of the outlay each year. The collection becomes self-supporting although it may take four or five years to become established.

It would be beyond reasonable expectation that everything will go right all the time. But in orchid growing a year is a very short period to elapse before a better result should appear.

How often a front-rank cattleya should produce top quality flowers is hard to predict, but about once in every four or five years would be a fair assessment. As good a reason for this as any other is inconsistent treatment by growers, quite apart from the prevailing weather outside enclosures.

Fertilisers, apart from being individual in constitution and regularity of application, are dealt with in *Growing Orchids, Book Two: The Cattleyas and Other Epiphytes*. For a formula for fertiliser, see chapter 3 above for cymbidium cultivation, and chapter 10 below.

All fertilisers are useless unless applied at the correct time and in correct strength. The root systems must be active and the plants receptive, and this occurs principally as new growths are maturing. This is when the quality of flowers is determined, not only after the buds begin to grow.

It is sometimes recommended that variations in the NPK ratios for flowering plants bring larger flowers. This is known as forcing and could have consequences which are best left out of specialist growing. It should be found better to continue with a well-balanced fertiliser for the whole collection where cattleyas are concerned. In the first place plants are usually in all stages of growth, maturing and flowering. A second and better reason is that too many mistakes are possible. By using a well-balanced fertiliser at a weak dilution there is little risk for plants which are unnecessarily sprayed or fertilised when they should be left without.

The system of using strong normal solutions of liquid nutrient followed later by heavy watering to flush the potting material is more applicable to commercial plant or flower harvesting than for smaller cultivators looking for the best results possible from the plants. The real needs of cultivated orchids for fertilisers when grown in containers are minute compared with earth-grown annuals, perennials or trees and shrubs.

For those used to the growth patterns of cymbidiums, the change into cattleya cultivation is like moving into another world. Cymbidiums grown in their natural climate seldom cease growing and produce flowers in season if they are not disturbed too frequently or severely. The two processes occur together. Cattleyas, as they are known, regardless of their inter-generic breeding, go through two definite stages—they grow and then they flower; they then appear to rest briefly in most instances before the cycle begins again. The two genera are totally different. Although some cymbidiums flower again from pseudo-bulbs once flowered, cattleyas, like most epiphytes, never flower twice from the same pseudo-bulb.

CATTLEYA COMPATIBLES

The same care in choosing any main genus to suit climates should be shown when selecting other genera to round out cattleya collections. Again the prevailing climate must be an influence.

Orchids with rank-growing habits which are greedy for space should be avoided. You should choose your 'fill-ins' for their neat habit and economy in using available space. After all, in spite of their probable attractiveness, they are only the icing on the cake.

With the return to species orchid growing in the bicentenary period it is possible to obtain a wide variety of orchids which suit the conditions for the three temperature ranges of cultivation.

It is not necessary to confine the choice to species: any hybrids which use space economically could be selected.

The principal flowering seasons of cattleyas are autumn and spring, although there are always some which fill in the odd months. But if possible it is a good idea to select genera which flower in winter or summer, so that when the cattleyas are absent there is something to stimulate interest.

The specialist collection would be incomplete without at least some of the *Cattleya labiata* group such as *C. trianaei* (Linden and Reichenbach) or *C. mossiae* (Hooker). Other genera such as *Laelia purpurata* (Lindley and Paxton), *Rhyncolaelia (Brassavola) digbyana* (Lindley) and cattleyas of the bifoliate section should be bought as they become available.

It should be noted that unless unlimited time and money are available the assembling of any worthwhile orchid collection cannot be easy or quick. It may take years and considerable patience to locate the plants and perhaps even then only in small propagations or mericlones. Preferably do not buy mericlones of species which have been planned abnormal varieties by the use of chemicals. Some of these subversions have been given varietal names which rightly should belong only to original natural species.

It is wise to join a club or society devoted to orchid-growing. It will help you to find avenues of supply, and a considerable amount of information is exchanged through them and between members.

BRASSOLAELIOCATTLEYAS
Brassolaeliocattleya
Emmon's Glacier (*Bc*
Deesse x *Lc* Jay Markell).
Provided the breeding line
for albino cattleyas is
followed there will be a
succession of this type of
flower. However, these
well-shaped whites also
have strong influence on
the breeding of coloured
cattleyas.

Brassolaeliocattleya
Liz Wright (*Lc* Elizabeth
Off x *Blc* Memoria Crispin
Rosales). An unnamed grex
carrying the vestiges of
'splash-petalled' breeding
lines somewhere. This type
of cattleya is eyecatching in
any orchid collection.

101

CATTLEYA LINKAGE
Cattleya Fascelis (*C. acklandiae* x *C. bicolor*). A hybrid raised by the Veitch establishment in 1900 which has stood the test of time. Both parents are bifoliates from Brazil. Many of the cross-pollinations made at the Veitch establishment were for the purpose of checking suspected linkages and natural hybrids. Some of these projects validated opinions held by botanists and non-botanists alike. Much is owed to the latter category of orchid growers.

Cattleya Victoria Regina (Linden and Reichenbach). The natural hybrid between the bifoliate *C. guttata* and *C. labiata* (Lindley). It was discovered originally by Louis Forget as a single specimen and was never plentifully dispersed. As a specialist subject it is unique and worth the search.

102

BIFOLIATE CATTLEYAS
Cattleya dormaniana
(Reichenbach f.).
A bifoliate found only in
Rio Janeiro state, Brazil.
It belongs to the same group
as *C. amethystoglossa*,
which has a restricted
habitat in Bahia, northern
Brazil.

Cattleya bicolor (Lindley).
This bifoliate could
perhaps be termed the
controlling member of
the group because its
habitats are widespread
over almost the whole of
Brazil. The colour is
variable from buff green
to the richness of this
specimen.

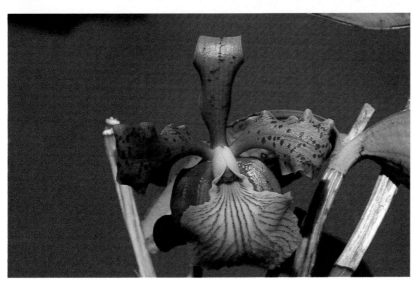

Cattleya velutina
(Reichenbach f.). One of
the most beautiful of the
bifoliates, it is rare in
cultivation and belongs
to the *C. bicolor* series.
Most of the bifoliates are
warm-growing, a notable
exception being
C. loddigesii (Lindley)
which appears on the front
of the book.

103

Laeliocattleya Puppy Love
(*C.* Dubiosa x *Laelia
anceps*). A delicately
beautiful specialist orchid,
remarkable for the use of
L. anceps (Lindley), which
never figured prominently
in cross-pollinations.
For intermediate climates
and doubtful in tropical
conditions. Most clones of
L. anceps are pink rather
than mauve.

Cattleya Porcia
(*C.* Armstrongiae x
C. bowringiana).
This variety was named
'Connisara' and has a blue
tinge which hybridisers
have sought to extend
throughout the entire
breeding program over
more than eighty years. So
far it has been evasive and
intensifying the blue tinge
has not been possible.

CLUSTER TYPE CATTLEYAS

Cattleya Chocolate Drop (*C. guttata* x *C. aurantiaca*) could be said to represent a facet of the 'revolution' which overtook the growing of cattleyas in the bicentenary period. It began, naturally, some years before the 1980 decade and was the equivalent of the extension of cymbidium cultivation into the miniature field. From the time of the first 'man on the moon' everything moved toward miniaturisation—a terrible but descriptive word.

The renewal of interest in the smaller species of many genera and their combination into sometimes experimental hybrids often met with success. But in all this success one of the attributes of most orchid flowers became important—their colour. In a critical examination of the flowers of *C.* Chocolate Drop in isolation as single blooms there is little remarkable about them. However, in their collective appearance as a 'cluster', which is the usual design-ation for these small cattleyas, there is a great amount of appeal.

A strange feature of this appeal is that it took so long to permeate the pastime, because *C.* Chocolate Drop was a production from the 1950 decade. It was followed by a succession of similar cross-pollinations using all the smaller species and following this into an inter-generic series such as the hawkinsaras, one of which is illustrated.

This cattleya and *C.* Priscilla Ward indicate the brilliance and difference which the bifoliate cattleyas introduced into collections. They are based on warm-growing species.

Cattleya Priscilla Ward
(*C. granulosa* x *C. forbesii*).
This is another example
of the use of the smaller
flowers from the bifoliate
or two-leafed section of
the genus, most members
of which come from Brazil.
There is a considerable
colour range in the
Brazilian section, which
includes the beautiful
and variable species
C. loddigesii (Lindley) and
C. intermedia (Graham),
both of which are
principally rose-pink to
almost lavender, and
include pure white or
albino varieties.

In the more unusual

colourings the species
frequently carry more
flowers and it was with the
idea of producing heads of
flowers which would
attract attention that the
hybridists set to work. As
with *C.* Chocolate Drop,
the intensity of breeding
occurred in the 1950
decade. Perhaps it should
be remarked that the
inspiration occurred much
earlier than that and it
was in this decade that
the results first became
apparent.

It should not be thought
that few or no similar
activities occurred before
that time, as the species

C. bowringiana (Veitch),
which also offered
prospects for these
attractive heads of flowers,
had been used for that
purpose as far back as the
beginning of the century.

In selecting these
cluster type cattleyas for
specialist collections, some
discrimination should be
shown. They should
preferably flower easily
and consistently and it
should be understood that
the results do not appear
quickly. Most of the plants
must be well grown for
periods of up to five years
before the ultimate is
reached.

106

SOPHRONITIS INFLUENCE
Sophrolaeliocattleya
Jewel Box (*C. aurantiaca* x
Slc Anzac) (above) is one
of the most brilliant of the
group and *Slc* Anzac even
more so. It was illustrated
in *Growing Orchids, Book
Two*, and is usually
regarded as the standard
by which to judge these
flowers. *Sophronitis
coccinea* was also
illustrated in *Growing
Orchids, Book Two*.

Sophrolaeliocattleya Tiger
Tears developed more of
the red of *S. coccinea* than
most of the group. An
intensified red is usually
sought by any orchid
specialist. *Potinara*
Gordon Siu, illustrated in
*Growing Orchids, Book
Two*, is probably the
ultimate.

107

OTHER INTER-GENERICS
Broughtonia sanguinea
(Swartz) Robert Brown.
The introduction of this
densely coloured little
Jamaican orchid into the
cattleya complex brought
a new race of miniatures.
As a cultivated plant
it is little known and
infrequently noted in
collections. The nature
of the climate in Jamaica
should never be a matter
of speculation, the word
Jamaica should be enough.
It is hot and frequently dry.

Cattleytonia (*C.* Hawaiian
Variable x *Ctna.*
Joy Bassin). An unnamed
grex which is a direct
contrast in colour, inherited
from both parents.
The cattleytonias have
a distinctive shape and
most measure about
5 centimetres across
(about 2 inches).

THE MERICLONE

Brassolaeliocattleya
Malworth 'Orchidglade'.
The three photographs are
of mericlone plants grown
by different people.
Perhaps it is best to ask
questions rather than
answer them. Is a
mericlone a perfect copy
of the original? Does the
cultivation of a cattleya by
different growers account
for such changes? How
much does variation of
seasons from one year to
another affect flower
quality? Is there a
difference in mericloning
procedures from one
processor to another?
Is there such a thing as
difference in the material
each propagator will use?
And the ultimate: Can a
true replica be expected
from material which has
itself been a mericlone
propagation?

There is no doubt that
many different answers
will be given by a cross-
section of orchid growers.
But the specialist must
give the subject a lot of
thought and grow a
number of plants before
some certainty will
emerge. As one who has
looked at thousands of
cattleyas with an
unfettered mind some of
the answers are very plain
indeed to the author.
Colour photography has
verified the conclusion
that our plants conform
to cultural and climatic
changes.

109

FROM EPICATTLEYA TO KIRCHARA

Epicattleya Aroma Grande (*Cattleya acklandiae* x *Encyclia cordigera*). The encyclia was once known as *Epidendrum atropurpureum*. For all purposes concerned with hybridising it is still an epidendrum and must remain so. This is one of the most beautiful of its hybridising history.

Kirchara (*Slc* Fiery Fantasy x *Epidendrum plicatum*), an unnamed grex. Again the complications of hyphenation or conglomerate words have been avoided and the shorter term kirchara used to designate the hybrids having sophronitis, laelia, cattleya and epidendrum in their program. There is very little indication of cattleya, laelia or sophronitis in the flowers.

110

Although Brazilian laelias are principally small flowered, there are more than forty for selection. In addition to *Laelia purpurata* (Lindley) the following should be at the head of the list of additions to cattleya collections.

Laelia perrinii (Lindley), light pink with a dark labellum, the pseudo-bulbs of which are about 30 centimetres high (about 12 inches) and the leaves about half as high again.

L. tenebrosa (Rolfe), a most unusual laelia, tan to dark brown-purple and once known in an orange-yellow form, growing to about the same height as *L. perrinii*.

L. xanthina (Lindley), variable, pale brownish-yellow to green-brown.

L. pumila (Hooker), frequently confused with *L. sincorana* (Schlechter), both of which are probably unsuitable for sub-tropical or tropical climates. This is a short, single-leafed orchid similar to a *labiata* cattleya.

L. lundii (Reichenbach f.), a beautiful miniature, white spotted with red-purple at times, with a brilliant purple-streaked labellum.

L. harpophylla (Reichenbach f.), orange to gold, with a small neat habit.

L. kautskyi (Pabst), gold. Habit also small and neat.

L. rupestris (Lindley), syn. *L. crispata* (Thunberg), small, pink. There are several laelias in a group similar to *L. rupestris* and the nomenclature is apparently confused, with such orchids as *L. oweniae* (with no authenticity) and *L. crispilabia* (A. Richard) indistinguishable. Pabst and Dungs also relegate *L. rupestris* (Lindley) to a synonym for *L. crispata* (Thunberg) Garay. In some ways the Brazilian section of the genus illustrates the chaos which can be caused by over-zealous taxonomists.

L. cinnabarina (Bateman) has been known and grown for more than a century, as the author's name indicates. While varying from clone to clone, it is generally tall-growing with a nice close-set rhizome and orange-red flowers.

L. flava (Lindley), chrome yellow flowers borne on tall stems.

L. longipes (Reichenbach f.), tall growing, the flowers pale cream to pink.

L. milleri (Blume), red to blood coloured, but not necessarily warm-growing like most of the Brazilian laelias. It was grown and flowered as a garden plant by the author in southern Victoria, yet also noted growing in a sub-tropical collection in open conditions.

L. jongheana (Reichenbach f.) belongs to the same group as *Laelia pumila* (Hooker, Reichenbach f.). It is pink and about the same size, with a pink labellum and yellow throat.

There are numerous lesser known orchids like the broughtonias, which are mostly native to Jamaica. The genus was named for Arthur Broughton, a botanist and *B. sanguinea* (Robert Brown) was one of the first orchids brought into cultivation in Britain, almost 200 years before this book was written. The broughtonias are rather hard-growing small orchids which would be very suitable as bright additions to cattleya collections, more particularly in warmer climates.

Laeliopsis domingensis (Lindley) was also once known as *Broughtonia lilacina*. It is closely related and comes from the same general area. Although both these miniature orchids are rare in cultivation they are worth an effort to get them.

There is considerable confusion attached to such members of the laelia family as *L. oweniae*, *L. latona* and *L. crispilabia*, because of taxonomic changes over the years which have not been carried into print sufficiently or when so appearing have been disregarded and older names retained.

This is something which taxonomists may find frustrating, but after looking at hundreds of orchid collections over the years, I find that names count for very little and that synonymy should be accepted far more readily than it appears to be. As far as possible within the time which may be allotted to books such as these only a certain amount of verification is possible and that when a certain point is reached I also become frustrated by taxonomists who apparently refuse to accept the work of their colleagues. It should not be inferred from this that as a writer I deprecate the work of taxonomists. On the contrary, I sympathise with them, but only in their handling of an almost impossible task of converting orchid growers to accepting something in which they display little interest.

Most laelias need to be sought outside Australia or through species orchid groups. International periodicals like the *Orchid Review*, the *Australian Orchid Review* or the *American Orchid Review* are the best advertising mediums to search for possible suppliers.

Leptotes bicolor (Lindley), a small Brazilian species allied to laelias and cattleyas, is another orchid which could be grown as a mid-climate subject in the glasshouse, preferably slab-mounted on cork or treefern. Other members of this genus may also become available.

The laelias listed are suited to a variety of growing situations from pot or container cultivation to slab mounting, and it is relatively easy to appreciate their dormant or growing phases when they are brought in as hanging plants rather than bench-grown.

Many of the group may be at risk flowering in highly humid conditions, an example being *L. sincorana* (Schlechter), which flowers on immature new summer growths prone to fungal infections. Natural climates are decisive in this regard and at the first signs of such infection it is better to sacrifice the new growth and flower, disinfect where possible with a good fungicide, and keep the plant dry about the foliage until the incisions and infections have hardened off. Good ventilation is usually enough to keep this sort of thing under control.

While it is possible to combine phalaenopsis with cattleyas in some climates, it is better not to integrate the two. One of them should take the major place in a collection, with the other as an addition. It is almost impossible to have this combination in any other than sub-tropical to tropical climates; to try it in temperate climates could prove disastrous and expensive, or at best unsatisfactory for one or the other.

One quite notable instance of successful integration of genera is given in the illustrations. It is outstanding and naturally situated in a tropical area of Australia, where the integration of many unusual orchids into one growing area is common, particularly in such a collection as that illustrated.

Calanthes may be suitable adjuncts to cattleya growing because they belong to a fast summer-growing list. They are among few genera which grow and flower from single pseudo-bulbs, were featured in *Growing Orchids, Book Three* and are not freely available. The potting mix can be fairly rich in humus. As the root system is impermanent and discarded as new pseudo-bulbs are made it should be high in fertiliser content, preferably organic. Calanthes should be repotted every year.

Calanthes cannot cope with the vagaries of the climate of southern Australia, where it is possible for a glasshouse to go from a daytime temperature of about 40 degrees Celsius (over 100 degrees Fahrenheit) to about 12 degrees Celsius (just over 50 degrees Fahrenheit) at night. No orchids of the calanthe group are accustomed to this wide variation and would produce only moderate flowering at best. If automation set to specialist standards is maintained a better result would follow, but even so it is possible the flowers would not be as large or the racemes as long as those on plants grown in the tropics.

Miniature orchids which can be grown as slab-mounted subjects hung against a wall in good light attract more notice than their often larger and more highly priced associates. The South African genera aeranthes, angraecum and aerangis suggest themselves, but they may be hard to get.

Another of these oddities is *Nageliella augustifolia* (Ames and Correll), from Guatemala. The plant itself is an untidy-looking clump, but the flowers, small and purple, are borne on long wiry stems which flower indefinitely. Few orchids possess the facility for producing flowers from the same stems in successive years and such plants are good additions to any orchid collection. It certainly offsets the sameness of cattleyas. *Nagelellia purpurea* (N. Williams) is equally attractive.

There is no reason why any of the terrestrial genera should not be fitted into warm-growing groups of orchids, but they will need a little more than ordinary care and would be entirely specialist in character.

In forming collections of species it is sometimes difficult to make decisions about the tolerance of different orchids. In such instances it is better to vary on the side of intolerance of cold rather than heat. For example, *Miltoniopsis roezlii* (Reichenbach f.) was originally found by Benedict Roezl, a noted collector of the mid-nineteenth century, floating down a river attached to a log. But let Roezl's story be told according to Veitch:

> Towards the end of March, 1873, I was going down the little river Dagua which flows into the Pacific Ocean. Like all the streams which flow into the ocean from the western Cordillera of New Granada, the current is rapid. I had reached to about ten miles from the outlet when my attention was arrested by the trunk of a tree that was being borne along down the stream upon which was an orchid, quite unknown to me, in full bloom. I immediately requested my negro to secure the treasure, a matter of considerable difficulty owing to the strength of the current. He at length succeeded in detaching the plants, three in number, from the log and which proved to be a new species of miltonia (odontoglossum), allied to *Miltonia vexillaria* and *M. phalaenopsis*. Some months later the plant [sic] with other novelties, was acquired by Mr William Bull, of Chelsea, for 250 francs.

The crux of the story, however, was that no particular habitat could be traced for the species, there was no indication of the climate in which it had been growing and, worse still, there was indeed some doubt cast on the reliance which could be placed on the actual location of the discovery, because the collectors of those days were notoriously elastic in their information of the how, where and when of their discoveries.

Others, including the collector Chesterton, later rediscovered the whereabouts of the source stock of Roezl's chance find, and this led to the ultimate appearance of the orchid in quantity in the collections of those days.

Francis Klaboch, a nephew of Roezl, later described the habitat, the plants of *M. roezlii* growing on trees and rocks, mostly in shady conditions, at 300 to 600 metres (about 1000 to 2000 feet) in Colombia, frequently in association with *Oncidium kramerianum* (Reichenbach f.). It is an orchid for a warm environment.

6 PAPHIOPEDILUMS: SPECIES OR HYBRIDS?

Ideally a choice should be made between species and hybrids when cultivating this genus, particularly if it is put together as a specialist collection in its own right.

It may seem odd to advocate this very different genus as an extension for a well-thought-out cattleya collection. But provided numbers are kept within sane limits it could work out very well. Either could be the major interest. The combination may not work in climates which periodically endure high temperatures combined

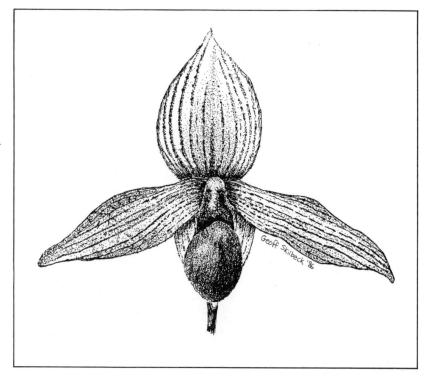

Paphiopedilum Delrosi
The parents of this primary hybrid, *P. delenatii* (Guillaumin) and *P. rothschildianum* (Reichenbach f.) Pfitzer, point up the trend of the bicentenary hybridising programme in the recombination of various species. *P.* Delrosi, however, was not an early hybrid and is of comparatively recent date. It is pink to red and could be an aid towards the rare pink colouration in hybrids of the genus. (A Geoffrey Skilbeck ink drawing)

with high humidity, where possibly some of the species Slippers may survive but few hybrids. Most of the species originate at cool altitudes even if they come from tropical countries, but a number have flexibility.

Having introduced them as compatible associates, there are certain differences in the relative needs of the two genera. Micro-climates can be used to good effect, but a primary consideration is their status—one genus is epiphytic, the other almost totally terrestrial in cultivation and with root systems which should not be allowed to dry out. To suit the two a growing area should be divided into sections. This can be done in two general ways, either careful design of benches and glasshouse or by partitioning off part of the structure. Neither system costs very much nor entails major

A divided glasshouse. One section is cold to cool and quite airy; the other is protected by an internal plastic film to increase warmth holding qualities. This protected area is treated individually for ventilation and supplementary heating.

reconstruction of existing enclosures. Plastic sheeting may be hung to form an internal wall. Thin as it is, the sheeting slows down or prevents the exchange of warm air for cold air to any extent. The flow is broken and tends to create circulation for itself in two or more compartments independently warmed. There are more problems in this system than in separate housing or benching and it is necessary or more beneficial to each genus to go through the same benching procedure on each side of the partition. Bench height can be varied, with one side of the enclosure having knee-high benching and that for cattleyas and other epiphytes hip high.

The illustrations in the chapter on micro-climates give clear views of types of benching suitable for cattleyas and for damp-growing genera such as paphiopedilums. The open-top bench gives the type of air flow epiphytes need because of their origins. The closed bench is of similar construction until the platform for the plants is fitted. In its simplest form it is surfaced with fibro-cement sheet and the edge, about 45 millimetres high (about 1¾ inches), can be formed with the plastic angle strip used to finish off the external corners of buildings. Both sheet and cornering are easy to buy at hardware suppliers or timber merchants.

Cutting the fibro-cement sheet to size may be a problem, but lacking a correct cutter an easy solution is illustrated on page 25. There is now no asbestos in cement sheeting.

The type of Slippers to be cultivated is a consideration. If species are to be grown they are better suited in small pots than in large, thus more plants can be fitted in. Species Slippers, which in a majority of instances are small by comparison with hybrid Slipper plants, do not now have a price advantage which they once had. As this book was being compiled, however, they were more easily disposed of or exchanged than hybrids.

One feature of species Slippers is extreme variation in quality of the flowers. Although there are some clones which have gained awards and are thus price adjusted, in general they tend to be held at a value on name only and not on any particular variety. A purchase of a species plant is a gamble; if it is an imported natural plant harvested from a habitat it could be good or bad and the chance must be taken.

A critical look should be taken at the temperature range in which species Slippers grow naturally. Their origins from various climates means that of the total catalogue of some sixty to seventy commonly available only about half should be expected to acclimatise and grow in the specific climate in which cattleyas thrive. Some are borderline, and species from cooler climates would be disadvantaged. Even if they survive they may regress and will not flower well.

THE PAPHIOPEDILUM

In the bicentenary period several new or comparatively new Slipper species have been introduced. This may appear surprising to cultivators of the genus, but if a longer term view is taken of the evolution and history of plants as a whole it may not seem all that unusual.

Paphiopedilum delenatii (Guillaumin) may serve as an example of the phenomenon. It could have been thought that with penetration by exploration and collection in such an area as Indo-China as a whole, which includes all the now separate states of the peninsula, that the plundering era of the centenary period would have accounted for all the orchids and few would have remained undiscovered. Almost a century elapsed from the discovery and cultivation of the first Slippers and the discovery and admiration of *P. delenatii* at the RHS Orchid Committee meeting in 1931 at which it was awarded a gold medal.

One very good reason why it was possibly overlooked was that the various collectors who visited those countries did so with particular orchids in mind and bypassed anything for which a certain market did not exist.

P. delenatii has always been something of a problem for cultivators, principally because it was treated as an addition to a collection without study of its habitat or the manner of its growth.

Appreciation of the individuality of all Slipper species in the bicentenary years has led to better treatment and results for this orchid, together with all the others which needed such consideration.

P. delenatii belongs to a singular group which has basic differences when compared with the Indo-Burmese Slippers such as *P. insigne* (Wallich) or *P. villosum* (Lindley), and unless these differences are allowed for the specialist cultivation of species Slippers as a whole becomes impossible.

Paphiopedilum charlesworthii (Rolfe) is among the more beautiful members of a strange genus.

This Slipper is no more difficult to grow than others, although it thrives less in cultivation than, say, *P. insigne* (Wallich). It originated in much the same area as that orchid, north-eastern India and Burma. *P. charlesworthii* possibly has more varieties than any other Slipper, a feature which was noted in early importations when it was introduced in the late years of the last century. Many of the most beautiful of these varieties have unfortunately been lost for all time, as the plants had a poor cultivated life. This has also been true of its history in other countries.

The *Orchid Review*, the official journal of British orchid growers, has been published almost continuously since January 1893. Colour reproduction is taken for granted in the latest issues of the journal, but its first volume included a colour reproduction of *P. charlesworthii* as a frontispiece. It was presented for the appreciation of the Orchid Committee of the Royal Horticultural Society in September of that year and was awarded a unanimous vote for a First Class Certificate. Perhaps time has dimmed its glamour, but for those fortunate enough to be able to grow

it well and flower it annually, it makes a very bright and beautiful spot in the glasshouse in late autumn.

Unfortunately the breeding history of the genus in hybrid form has been clouded by carelessness and wrong names, but there is little doubt that the colour of *P. charlesworthii*, which varies from almost pure white to the deepest maroon reds, has been passed on to many of the prized possessions of modern growers.

Paphiopedilum callosum (Reichenbach f.). Much of the history of this Slipper was given in *Growing Orchids, Book One.* Since its discovery in 1885, at which time it was introduced to horticulture, several other similar Slippers have come into cultivation which are modifications or natural divergences of a common theme in plant morphology. Like most sections of the genus, it appeared to have developed in the Indo-China area.

P. callosum was never as frequently cultivated or mentioned in print as other well-known Slippers, the exception being the mutation in green and white which was responsible for a beautiful section of the hybrid genus. However, with its closely related species *P. barbatum* (Lindley) and *P. lawrenceanum* (Reichenbach f.) it has also produced very beautiful hybrids with the typical shape of the section. Where in the second century of Slipper cultivation the move has been consistently towards producing a rounded hybrid flower, toward the end of that period a move was made back to cross-pollination of the *P. callosum* type of flower. In the process some of the most beautiful paphiopedilums were produced in *P.* Vintner's Treasure and *P.* Goultenianum, which was the result of the 1894 cross-pollination of *P. callosum* and *P. curtisii* (Reichenbach f.).

All the coloured forms of these Slippers have some red as a basic attribute and the astute hybridists worked through the breeding lines to intensify the proportion of red. Perhaps it is better and easier to ask the question than to answer it: why is this colour so eagerly sought by so many orchid growers?

Paphiopedilum curtisii
(Reichenbach f.).
A Sumatran species
originating at about 1000
to 1500 metres. Altitude,
however, is not always a
reliable guide and this
Slipper could not thrive
in cool to cold climatic
cultivation. It should be
considered for warmer-
grown collections,
particularly of a specialist
nature.

The foliage of many
paphiopedilums is very
beautiful, rivalling that of
some plants grown for this
feature. Glossy, healthy
foliage is usually an
indicator for good
flowering.

An example of this, although in a reverse pattern, could be found in *Paphiopedilum venustum* (Wall ex Sims). This orchid is generally considered to be cool-growing, yet occasional plants thrive in sub-tropical temperatures in association with other orchids.

The warmer climate Slippers include:

Paphiopedilum acmodontum (Schoser ex Wood), which is quite variable, with some plants available suggesting they are natural hybrids generated from *P. ciliolare* (Reichenbach f.).

P. appletonianum (Rolfe). Taxonomists over a period have had their way with this Slipper and its obvious affiliates are very close in appearance.

P. argus (Reichenbach f.). Usually unmistakeable with its intense spotting.

P. barbatum (Lindley). A number of these plants appear to be rather drab replicas of the red forms. If specialising, be selective and buy on sight where possible.

P. bullenianum (Reichenbach f.).

P. callosum (Reichenbach f.). This is most variable depending on the origin of plants. Some are more delicately coloured. Flower size is fairly constant. This Slipper can be very frustrating, and lack of success should cause you to dispose of it.

P. ciliolare (Reichenbach f.). There is a marked difference in forms of this Slipper and a lack of information on the true type if printed information is any guide.

P. curtisii (Reichenbach f.). There is a marked difference in the best and poorer varieties. Choose carefully.

P. delenatii (Guillaumin). More romantic stories have been woven around this than any other species Slipper. Not all of them are true. The orchid has the reputation of being a difficult subject, but the truth is probably that the grower rather than the plant is difficult.

P. elliottianum (O'Brien). Originally named after Elliott, an American nurseryman, according to Veitch's *Manual*. It appeared as a variant of *P. rothschildianum* according to Rolfe. It was little known for some sixty years, but has reappeared in the 1980s, occasionally under the name *P. laevigatum* which is incorrect.

P. exul (O'Brien). Variable. Very glossy golden yellow in its best form. A very hardy Slipper, after the fashion of *P. insigne* (Wallich).

P. glanduliferum (Blume). A tropical species which should be cultivable in most climates. An apparently adaptable species from a fairly wide area and varying altitudes. Sometimes sold under its synonym of *P. praestans* (Reichenbach f.).

P. haynaldianum (Reichenbach f.). A very strong-growing Philippines Slipper, first brought to cultivation between 1870 and

1875. It grows at all altitudes up to 1000 metres, mostly on limestone country. A very beautiful species, multiple flowered.

P. hookerae (Reichenbach f.). This orchid was discovered in Borneo and named in 1863 and is comparatively rare in cultivation.

P. laevigatum. Considered conspecific with *P. philippinense*, which was named by Reichenbach after being introduced by John Gould Veitch in 1864.

P. lowii (Lindley). To quote Veitch's *Manual:* 'Discovered in Sarawak in north-west Borneo growing on high trees in thick jungle and flowering in April and May, by Sir Hugh Low.' It was subsequently collected in quantity in the same area when found growing in thick clumps in the forks of trees and often at great height from the ground. Unlike many of the genus, *P. lowii* should be regarded as an epiphyte rather than the terrestrial orchid the genus is generally taken to be. Some may dispute the use of the word terrestrial for the genus, but this is the cultivation program.

P. mastersianum (Reichenbach f.). This Slipper was collected from the Sunda Straits region and first sent to the Kew Gardens, where it flowered and was named after Dr M. T. Masters, editor of the *Gardeners' Chronicle*. It is illustrated in *Growing Orchids, Book One*.

P. papuanum (Ridley). There is still no satisfactory alignment of this species with others from contiguous land masses and known by various other names. It is a unique type and quite distinct from other Asian-Pacific paphiopedilums.

P. rothschildianum (Reichenbach f.). Originally introduced to cultivation by Mr Jean Linden and named *Cypripedium neo-guineense* but never registered as such in the requisite way. It was subsequently correctly titled in honour of Baron Ferdinand de Rothschild, an English parliamentarian.

P. stonei (Hooker f.). This species grows in a habitat which is possibly the direct opposite to that of *P. lowii*. The plant is almost lithophytic, in company with other members of the genus, and the contrast of the different root systems and their treatment in cultivation is described in the chapter on root systems.

P. sukhakulii (Schoser-Senghas), *P. tonsum* (Reichenbach f.), and *P. charlesworthii* (Rolfe) are illustrated and described in *Growing Orchids, Book One*, together with *P. parishii* (Reichenbach f.), *P. spicerianum* (Reichenbach f.), *P. fairrieanum* (Lindley), *P. venustum* (Wallich ex Sims), *P. hirsutissimum* (Lindley ex Hooker) and its darker counterpart *P. esquirolei* (Schlechter); *P. villosum* (Lindley).

A totally different group of paphiopedilums, with regard to methods of culture, could be based on *P. bellatulum* (Reichenbach f.) as the superior member. The section includes *P. concolor* (Bateman), *P. godefroyae* (Godefroy), and *P. niveum* (Reichenbach f.). *P. delenatii*, already mentioned, should be considered as another member. All these Slippers come from a compact sector of Indo-Asia based principally on the Indo-Chinese peninsula, and could well have derived from a common ancestor in the remote past.

Another complete and different group of Slippers coming from the southern extension of that sector is formed about a principal member originally named *P. chamberlainianum*. The name of the consolidated section is *P. victoria regina* (Sander) (M. Wood) and it is described in *Growing Orchids, Book One*. Its cultivation, while not singular, must take account of a very extended flowering season from the same spike or raceme over a period of months in the best of conditions. The authors of the complex are too confused to detail here.

Full details of consolidation of several similar species under the general title *P. victoria regina* (Sander) (M. W. Wood) can be found in the *Orchid Review* for May 1976. The original name *P. victoria mariae* (Hooker f.) Rolfe was superseded and is a doubtful synonym. Alex Hawkes has one version which is dissimilar to that of Wood, who expresses the basionym as *P. victoria regina* (Sander) in the *Gardeners' Chronicle* of 13 February 1892.

The specialist may well consider the confusion which has been caused by various authorities in the naming of the related genera paphiopedilum, phragmipedium and cypripedium, the spelling of which could well be out of date by the time this book is printed.

In the *Gardeners' Chronicle* of 9 September 1899, the following appeared under the heading 'Orchid Notes and Gleanings'.

REVISION OF THE CYPRIPEDIEAE

One of the most interesting features in our contemporary botany is certainly the revision of the Cypripedieae group, which was and still is the subject of many scientific discussions. Several great authorities undertook and discussed the matter and I am pleased to bring forward in recognition of their valuable classification the names of Prof. Pfitzer, of Heidelberg, the well-known German Botanographer, and our good friend Mr R. A. Rolfe, F.L.S., of the Kew Herbarium, to whom the Orchid world is so much indebted for his special studies and monographs, amongst which 'The Morphological and Systematic Review of the Apostasieae' forms one of the most interesting records in connection with these notes.

This well-known group of Linnaeus was in recent years divided into distinct sections or sub-groups. One of the first attempts was made in 1886 by Prof. Pfitzer and established in 1888. This new method of classification was not immediately adopted. However, it must be stated that its bases were to divide the Cypripedium group into distinct genera from a scientific, geographical and horticultural point of view.

This idea was not practically new, for Lindley in 1842 anticipated the necessity of separating the Indian species from their Western allies, although botany and horticulture have for another half a century kept under the same determination plants greatly different in habits, structure and origin. In 1894 the discussion was revived and has since reached a definite result.

When Comte Oswald de Kerchove de Denterghem, President of the Royal Agricultural and Botanical Society of Ghent, published his valuable book on Orchids, *Le Livre des Orchidees*, he adopted Prof. Pfitzer's classification, which gave rise to interesting criticisms in all the leading European papers.

Time has given proof of the above necessity and Mr R. A. Rolfe undertook the subject and brought it to its present standard.

Linnaeus established in 1737 a special genus on a well-known European species (*Cypripedium calceolus*) and called it Cypripodium, a determination composed of Kupris, one of the synonyms of Venus, and podion, small foot. Later on this became the subject of a slight alteration by the substitution of a single letter, which produced Cypripedium. Here we have the exact origin of that familiar name. But this did not describe Linnaeus' idea, which was, according to the traditions of botany, the translation of 'Venus' Slipper'. Podion, as selected by the author, was perfectly right; but pedion means plain or level (or a small chain). This shows the defective alteration which has become so widely used in practice which it would be extremely difficult to correct now.

In 1892 Prof. Pfitzer, in his classification of Orchids, separated the tribe into three sections. The first included our old species, remarkable for their one-celled ovary. He called these Cypripediums, with thin teguments to the seed. Secondly, the Selenipedium group was distinguishable by its three-celled ovary deeply marked with the crustaceous teguments of the seed. The third group was composed of species having the three-celled ovary, with thin teguments, and was called Paphiopedilum, another derivation of 'Venus' Slipper'. This last generic name has been modified in the latest classification and remains now Paphiopedium. Mr R. A. Rolfe, with his authority on the matter, pointed out several overlooked mistakes and undertook the complete revision of the Cypripedieae tribe, basing his classification on the nature of the ovary and on the disposition of the seeds therein, which obliged the author to divide the tribe into four distinct genera, which are all characteristic of their own peculiarities. In the following classification Selenipedium are reduced to only three species. Phragmopedium of Rolfe unites Reichenbach's Selenipedium with coriaceous leaves with the Phragmopedium of Pfitzer.

This is sufficient to explain the origin of the three generic names

Paphiopedilum fowliei (Birk). A comparative newcomer to the genus as it was finally named in 1981. This attractive Philippines species grows as a semi-terrestrial at about 700 metres (over 2000 feet). It should therefore acclimatise to milder tropical climates.

Paphiopedilum javanicum (Reinw.) (bottom left). This orchid is named for the island where it was discovered by the botanist Reinwardt in 1826, growing at about 1500 metres. The climate at this altitude would be cool, but this Slipper would not be a subject for that form of cultivation. Possibly it would fit well into an intermediate system.

Paphiopedilum laevigatum (Bateman) (below), the correct name of which is *P. philippinense* (Reichenbach f.). It is also known as *P. roebbelenii*. The genus is no exception when it comes to names and the history is confused. This Slipper occurs as a variable orchid in areas of the Philippine Islands.

Paphiopedilum rothschildianum (Reichenbach f.). One of the most attractive Slippers. It has been found in Borneo and, according to some authorities, in New Guinea. Originally brought to cultivation about 1887 by Sander and Linden, not in conjunction, it is strikingly handsome, bearing two or more flowers. It should be suitable for tropical cultivation with the usual reservations.

Paphiopedilum urbanianum (Fowlie). A Philippine Islands species from a relatively low altitude. It is remarkably similar to other Slipper species from the Burma-Philippines-Sumatra triangle, which contains the probable original habitats of the genus. Some people contend that this region saw the evolution of orchid genera as a whole, but it seems unlikely.

128

Paphiopedilum hookerae
(Reichenbach f.). A Sabah,
northern Borneo species,
commonly found growing
at about 1000 metres (more
than 3000 feet). It is not
cool-growing, although
the area of its habitat is not
tropical. The environment
counts for more than
altitude and is not easy to
simulate in a mixed
collection.

*Paphiopedilum
volonteanum* (Sander).
Another Slipper from
Borneo. The relationship
between it and *P. hookerae*
is quite obvious,
something which occurs
commonly in the
Philippine-Malaysia-Java
triangle. It is informative
to read the text of Helen
Valmayor's *Orchidiana
Philippiniana* on the
genus, particularly in the
matter of acceptable
nomenclature.

129

Paphiopedilum armeniacum. This beautiful addition to the genus comes more than 150 years after the discovery and naming for cultivation of *P. venustum* (Wallich), in 1820. *P. armeniacum* belongs to a small group of Slippers which originates in southern China and about which nothing was known. It is singular, like the other members of the group, yet is different in some ways from its co- member *P. micranthum.* At the base of the petals behind the staminode there is a fairly dense mat of pale hairs, quite long on some varieties and indistinct on others. This is one of eight photographed and the largest of the eight. The dorsal is rather insignificant, but the colour most attractive. The foliage is brilliantly tesselated in dark and light green in a fine patterning.

Cypripedium japonicum (Thunberg) var. *formosanum.* An Asian-Japanese member of the cypripediloideae. The genus is found only in the northern hemisphere and at the beginnings of orchid growing was a common field or forest flower. This flower was produced in a specialist collection, but in general the cypripediums are cool-climate orchids and not particularly easy to grow.

Phragmipedium schlimii (Bateman). The phragmipediums are the southern hemisphere branch of the total family, all growing in South America. They are separated from the paphiopedilums and cypripediums by an enormous gap in time and space. *P. schlimii* is a Colombian species and one of the most attractive of the group. Cross-pollinations with paphiopedilums produced plants, but very few ever flowered.

which are now current. It also explains why some members of the genus have an author's name followed by that of Pfitzer, such as *Paphiopedilum lawrenceanum* (Reichenbach f.) Pfitzer. Most of the species names such as *P. lawrenceanum* were in use almost as soon as the plants were discovered and brought into cultivation, but they could have been known as cypripediums and not paphiopedilums. The generic name was botanically notified and registered by Professor Pfitzer or at least credited to him in 1886. There are others such as 'Rolfe' or 'Stein' and the same indicators are common where species names remain as first registered or described and orchids have been removed to other classifications.

Several other species paphiopedilums were noted and illustrated in *Growing Orchids, Book One* and there is sufficient information available in current literature about them. They include the commoner forms of *P. insigne* (Wallich), *P. villosum* (Lindley) and *P. spicerianum* (Reichenbach f.). All these Slippers and others named before the changes in nomenclature just referred to are entitled to have included in their authority the name Pfitzer in recognition of the man who detailed their classification under the new regime. Robert Allen Rolfe made later adjustments.

It will be noted, in referring to *Growing Orchids, Book One*, that the spelling in many instances has been changed. This is to conform to the many taxonomic changes which have occurred since that book was published. No doubt there will be many more if taxonomic changes are persisted with.

In recent years several notable discoveries have been made in the genus and some plants would be better described as variants of known species or natural hybrids. But it is remarkable that the natural world still has something new to offer man while he so assiduously seeks to destroy that which he already has.

Among these 'new' paphiopedilums are species which have been known as growing in areas like southern China yet have never been collected in quantity for cultivation. The strange parallel exists of the relatively poor residents of this part of the world (and their counterparts in South America) suddenly coming to realise the value of their native plants as trade goods for exchange with entrepreneurs from other countries. It is as such trade goods that these new Slippers are slowly coming to the hands of growers in various countries. They were very expensive trade goods as this book was being compiled, with *Paphiopedilum micranthum* illustrated in the *Orchid Review* of May 1986. At sight this Slipper could almost be regarded as the 'missing link' in the triple conglomerate of the cypripediloideae.

So far we have been considering paphiopedilums as adjuncts to cattleya collections, but it is possible to assemble a worthwhile collection of the genus in species and hybrid forms to satisfy the most ardent specialist. It is equally possible to form complete collections on the same terms using only species and their varieties as the base.

As always, the success of the project would depend primarily on external climatic conditions, with experience suggesting that temperate to milder sub-tropical climates may be the best possibilities. Even at this point climate dividing lines limit the combinations.

Where the temperature in hotter parts of the year exceeds 35 degrees Celsius (about 95 degrees Fahrenheit) for any period beyond a day or two, and the humidity is high, many species would fail. Hybrids would have a tolerance level some degrees lower than that. Climate modifiers such as evaporative coolers would scarcely be able to cope with such conditions. If you live in such a climate it would be better to abandon the idea of a paphiopedilum and cattleya combination, and consider other genera such as smaller vandaceous elements. You would need to allow for the extra space required by larger orchids, but as construction costs are slightly less for open type enclosures the only limiting factor would be space.

The recommendation for a different combination in warmer climates is based on the fact that although many orchid species originate at tropical altitudes of 1000 to 2000 and more metres (about 3200 to 6500 feet), at these elevations the climate is fresh and cool for many months, particularly at night. The high temperatures and high humidity associated with lower altitudes and down to sea level where many paphiopedilum species grow are comparatively rare at the higher level.

In specialising to the degree outlined here, the symptoms of failure would be slow leaf growth and a general unhealthy aspect typified by lax foliage. The leaves should appear glossy and fresh at all times. If they do not, it is probable that the plants should not have been included in the environment provided. Insufficient analysis was made of the conditions under which the plants were supposed to grow. The contributing factor of incorrect potting material could be common in failures and an examination of root systems may confirm whether this is a cause.

Gross overcrowding (not to be confused with the natural liking of the plants for contact growing) and also two-tier or three-tier arrangements or other constrictions completely negate any prospects for specialist culture.

If hybrid paphiopedilums are chosen as an adjunct to a main genus, their intrinsic value is not as important as when they form a total collection. As a minor part of an orchid collection they could be chosen for their looks more than conformity to rigorous award qualifications. In this sense also it may be difficult to keep up with developments and trends. Although the genus is in an advanced stage of hybridising in fifteen or more generations of development and the requirements are almost fulfilled, there could still be some surprises in colour or a change in appreciation.

In the middle years of the 1980 decade as this book was being compiled the mericloning of paphiopedilums had defeated science and the entrepreneurs alike. In morphological terms it should be possible to clone these orchids just like any others and perhaps the solution is not that far away. But in the present regime it is still a matter of buying seedlings, discarding those with undesirable qualities and slowly building an individual collection. If you succeed in this, the best plants should not be divided into general cultivation or given to your best friends, but rather retained in specialist collections.

The metamorphosis of the genus into its present form has entailed cross-pollination of almost the whole of the known paphiopedilum range. To estimate the number of cross-pollinations is impossible because so many are never registered. But of those registered the majority have long since been culled and the stage has been reached where primary cross-pollinations are again being raised, principally as novelties, with no thought of following similar lines with reselected parents. Like all other genera which have periodic popularity, the paphiopedilum has about run its course in the 1980s.

Some of the simpler modifications recommended for growing the genus are given in chapter 11, the section about Slippers which refers particularly to cultivation in warmer areas.

7 ODONTOGLOSSUMS

The odontoglossum referred to in the heading of the chapter could be a combination of all the species of odontoglossums, cochliodas, miltonias and occasionally other species used in cross-pollinations to produce flowers which look like the true odontoglossum species, in the same way as cattleya has been used to define a whole galaxy of hybrids which look like cattleyas.

This genus in its entirety is diverse and the South American content something of a puzzle. In cultivation it is the cool-growing equivalent of phalaenopsis and it must be understood thoroughly for what it is—an epiphyte which is not dictated to by seasonal changes. It has no annual pattern in the hybrid form; it is intolerant of dryness and equally intolerant of exposure to heat. In fact, it is the direct opposite of most tropic-based orchid growing.

Among the first orchids which the author grew was a plant of the first odontioda raised and named. It fired my imagination, and the attraction to the odontoglossum has never deserted me from sight of that first plant. It led in turn to other odontoglossums and the sometimes bitter lessons that orchid growing brings to most people in their salad days. It was not until I had studied the plants and absorbed the material available that an understanding of the necessities of life for the conglomerate group was finally burned into my brain. They were different. They did not conform to the rules. They flowered when it suited them. They were never inactive for longer than a week or so at a time.

The full detail of their evolution as a genus in the *Odontoglossum crispum* section is impossible to unravel, but early cultivators such as described in *Growing Orchids, Book Two*, backed up by men of such stature as Robert Allen Rolfe, contributed most of the knowledge of the present day. Painstakingly they pieced together a pattern by which to identify the elements. They added material to

THE ODONTOGLOSSUMS
Odontoglossum crispum
(Lindley) var. *aureum.*
The conception of this
species as being always
white with perhaps a few
markings is mistaken.
It is very colourful.
The Colombian genus
has interbred to a degree
which can only be guessed
at. A pure white form was
illustrated in *Growing
Orchids, Book Two.*
This is a crayon drawing
by Margaret Skilbeck taken
from an old catalogue
issued at the end of the
nineteenth century and
part of the author's library.

Odontoglossum coradinei
(Reichenbach f.).
A natural hybrid between
Odm. crispum (Lindley)
and *Odm. lindleyanum*
(Reichenbach f.), also a
Margaret Skilbeck drawing
from the same source.
There were a large
number of natural hybrids
among importations of the
genus and these were
usually verified by later
cross-pollinations made
by various cultivators
including the Veitch
establishment, a principal
distributor of imported
plants. Many of these
verifications are recorded
in *The Orchid Stud Book,*
by Rolfe and Hurst (1909).

135

Cochlioda noezliana or *noetzliana* (Reichenbach f.). A native of Peru, member of a small genus and first introduced to Europe about 1890, the collector unrecorded with any accuracy. Among the orchid species generally there are several which have had tremendous influence on hybridising. *C. noezliana* is one of these, without which much of the colour of the odontoglossum complex would be absent.

Odontioda Wimmera (*Oda.* Matanda x *Oda.* Haniesto). A good example of the interbreeding of the two genera. Most odontoglossums are cool growing, the cochliodas from slightly warmer climates, and *Cochlioda noezliana* the most handsome of the genus. A further move to make the odontoglossums more tolerant for warmer climates was outlined in *Growing Orchids, Book Two* by the introduction of aspasias to the breeding program.

Cochlioda rosea (Lindley). Slightly smaller than *C. noezliana* and less frequently noted. It is a specialist orchid which should feature in collections of various species, but is not cold-growing, nor is it suited to warmer regions.

Odontioda Abigail 'Vaila'
This grex is remarkable
for its inclusion of
Odontoglossum rossii
(Lindley) as one of the
parents. Normally this
small Mexican and Central
American species could be
expected to be dominant.
However, the overriding
influence of *Cochlioda
noezliana* (Reichenbach f.)
Rolfe produces good
colouration. (A Geoffrey
Skilbeck ink drawing)

the conviction of men of an earlier decade, such as Bentham, who doubted that there was any such thing as a true species. So far as the 1980 decade is concerned one cannot be anything other than amused at the people who rush about finding new species all the time. They are rather late on the scene. Perhaps they fail to recognise that the process is continuous or they hope to be noted by posterity.

The early growers of odontoglossum species worked out a complex temperature table for cultivation and flowering, also for other genera.

The odontoglossums, like most of the orchids of both hemispheres, were ruthlessly plundered and destroyed. The gene pool is perhaps not entirely lost, but it is beyond probability that some of the forms illustrated in this book still survive.

Read on and understand.

Although the geographical range of *O. crispum* is comparatively limited, there is a marked difference in the varieties found in various localities. The Pacho mountains are the home of the finest forms and here the plants grow on the lower branches of the forest trees in company with *O. gloriosum* and *O. lindleyanum*, two inferior species in point of beauty, but which have perhaps in a great measure been instrumental in producing the beautiful narrow petalled supposed hybrids such as Andersonianum, Ruckerianum, Jenningsianum and others. It is peculiar that, whereas the starry flowered forms similar to Lindley's specimen abound exclusively on the north of Bogota, the woods on the south, about ten days' journey distant, are rich in the fine round-flowered varieties. Although this orchid is imported in larger numbers than any other from South America, the risks and expenses are not slight even now. In our case, we purchase the exclusive rights to collect plants in the woods in certain districts; natives are employed to gather them, for which purpose parties of from four to eight go into the woods, returning in about a fortnight with the result of their labour. After the plants have been cleaned and prepared and kept on wooden stages for several weeks they are ready for packing. They are then fastened to stout sticks and these are fixed in wooden boxes so as to leave air space around them. The cases are carried on muleback to Bogota, a journey of about ten days and here they are received by an agent, who sends them by mules to Honda, which is reached in another six days. The place is situate on the river Magdalena, and here the cases are put on board a river steamer, which takes them to the seaport town of Savanilla, a journey occupying about five days. Owing to the intense heat on the river journey the plants often perish. The cases then come as a rule by mail steamer via Colon and St. Thomas to England, the passage being made in about 27 days. The risks, therefore, of importing this orchid are great, and owing to the peculiarly soft nature of the plants they are so liable to decay that in some instances seven-eighths of the consignment is dead on arrival here. The havoc made in the native forests, too, must be considerable, for we calculate that for every three plants actually established in European gardens a tree has been felled.

Thus Frederick Sander, writing in *Reichenbachia* published in 1888, in reference to *Odontoglossum crispum* (Lindley), which was also known at one period as *Odontoglossum alexandrae* (Bateman).

For committed orchid growers there is something terribly poignant and final in that quotation. In almost one hundred years it appears that human nature has changed little and we have learned nothing. Precisely the same thing is happening to what is still left of the world's riches in flora. It may be more appropriate for time and energy to be committed to saving the remnant, instead of concentrating on what name it should bear and whether it should be printed in italic type.

In the cool to cold climates of Britain and Europe in which orchid growing commenced, emphasis was always on creating warmth rather than on cooling the growing environments. In these conditions basic rules were formulated and many of these rules are relevant to the total cult. For example, the summer recommendations for a cool environment suggest a constant daytime temperature of 15 degrees Celsius (about 60 degrees Fahrenheit) and a night minimum of about 10 degrees (about 50 degrees Fahrenheit).

It was in such environments that the cool-growing genera like odontoglossums were cultivated. It should be pointed out, however, that the complex interbreeding of cochlioda, miltonia and oncidium in combination with odontoglossum species or hybrids had not then occurred, and the flexibility of such hybrids was not appreciated. As they appear in the bicentenary period many hybrids will tolerate quite high daytime temperatures, provided they have adequate air flow to cool them and humidity to modify temperatures of 25 degrees Celsius (about 80 degrees Fahrenheit) and upward.

But this statement must be qualified. Such temperatures must be only occasional; anything more than a day or two of such unnatural heat could soon end odontoglossum growing. The conglomerate odontoglossum in its present form is as inconsistent as the so-called cattleya.

A table of recommendations in its total form would indicate a daytime temperature of about 18 degrees Celsius (about 65 degrees Fahrenheit) and a night temperature of 13 to 16 degrees Celsius (about 55 to 60 degrees Fahrenheit) for what is known as an intermediate collection of orchids, which included cattleyas. For such things as vandas and phalaenopsis, in the warm sector, the daytime temperature recommended is 22 to 27 degrees Celsius (about 70 to 80 degrees Fahrenheit) and for night time about 16 to 18 degrees Celsius (about 60 to 65 degrees Fahrenheit).

All these temperatures were minimums, below which orchids in the different categories were at risk. The peaks of higher temperatures were not quoted at all and misconception arose over this point. For example, the maximum daytime temperatures in which cultivation of cool-growing orchids was possible could be quite variable within safe limits and for periods which were not prolonged.

These growing conditions were arrived at in the nineteenth century in establishments comprising a number of glasshouses or enclosures, such as the group illustrated on page x, in which it was possible to move plants about to various environments. Incidental to this movement, it was frequently found that plants from tropical countries responded better to intermediate or cool conditions than the warmth to which they were first exposed. Most growers of today do not have these facilities and must be more careful about committing themselves to grow particular orchids.

With regard to ventilation and air flow, which are two distinct things, the original recommendation for a cool climate stated that nearly all orchids from hill and mountain country should have fresh air fully admitted on all possible occasions, particularly in glasshouses in cool to intermediate climates. Today's growers are able to separate ventilation from airflow by means of forced ventilation, which is one of the most important factors of orchid-growing in the late 1980s. Even when ventilation is almost closed off, the air should be constantly passed across the plants. There are many different circulating fans available some of which make it possible to introduce warm air through space heaters, to mix outside and recirculated inside air, or use total ambient air with no temperature controls operating. With all the controls available, a certain amount of automation is possible. But even in its most sophisticated form an automated system cannot produce the same results as personal contact with the plants. The use of modern equipment should not be looked on as a lazy way to grow orchids. Some of it is illustrated in this book and also in the others of the series. But for specialist growing it should not be relied on too heavily. The systems of control are designed also for cool-growing orchids such as odontoglossums and masdevallias, which are only two of many genera in the category. They also need air flow and occasional warmth in cold climates.

By contrast, in the nineteenth century, in what were known as the stove or East Indian sections devoted to warm-growing orchids and other plants, air could not be admitted freely. Personal control on almost a 24-hour basis was needed to hold the balance. This was maintained in some of the larger establishments like that illustrated, where it was possible because of the large number of gardeners and labourers employed. But there was also a great deal of devotion and sense of duty in the committed people who grew the plants. It was an honour indeed to be known as 'Mr So-and-so's grower'.

Odontoglossums, so-called, are ideal orchids for cooler climates, but for several reasons they are not cultivated as much as their beauty and easy growing capabilities would suggest. Poor availability of plants, compared with cymbidiums and other commoner genera, is one reason and another is trepidation about spending money on them. But such hesitancy is foolish. Within reason they are among the easiest of orchids to grow.

To grow odontoglossums successfully, it is necessary to plan for them as a main genus, instead of having a plant or two as fill-ins, which is customary with so many other orchids. The planning must be based on provision of moisture, low temperature, and a fresh atmosphere. It could be imagined that with those minimum requirements they would be easy orchids to combine with other cool-growing things such as some of the Slippers, but in reality odontoglossums generally are poor mixers.

A total enclosure is not always necessary in moderate climates, but for such as that of southern Australia, with its ups and downs from day to day, it is best to start off with a glasshouse which offers correct light, preferably morning sunlight from as close to sunrise as possible.

There are three possible designs for glasshouses suitable for odontoglossum culture. A skillion-roof design such as that illustrated on page 94 should face to the south with the path against the wall of the north side. A glasshouse which has its roof longer on one side should have the long side to the south and have at least half a metre of glass (about 20 inches) in the upper part of the south wall. A north–south gable-roofed house should be benched in such a way that 'odontoglossums' are grown on the east side, with the western side of the roof providing heavier shade from after-noon sun.

If correctly shaded, the foliage of 'odontoglossums' will be mid-green to darker. If it is light coloured or has a red tinge, the plants are getting too much light. Most of the genus in its hybrid form is descended from tolerant species, but hybrids with mixed parentage of odontoglossum, cochlioda and oncidium still appear to carry the odontoglossum characteristic of pale foliage easily damaged by the sun. They are hardy to a degree, but once the shade barrier is broken down too far they react quickly.

Air flow in such glasshouses or enclosures should not be confined to recirculation, even in cold weather. Inflow, however small, should be introduced all the time.

There should always be an outflow of air through upper venti-lators; it is not advisable to blow the air back down on the plants with a downdraught fan in the angle of the roof. The idea is to keep the system as natural as possible by emulating the habitats of most of the species involved, which for odontoglossums, the dominant genus in the combinations, is cool to cold and with rising air circulation.

In the event of air temperature rising above about 25 degrees Celsius (about 72 degrees Fahrenheit), some cooling by evaporation and air flow is essential, although it is not the death-line for these plants.

Odontoglossums are cool-climate epiphytes which grow in light cloud forest conditions. *Cochlioda noezliana* (Reichenbach f.) is an epiphyte with slightly better tolerance. Oncidiums are such a varied habitat genus that no true idea of their effect on the hybrid odontoglossum is discernible in their tolerance. They certainly do not inherit the temperature tolerance of such as *Oncidium tigrinum* (La Llave-Lexarza), a Mexican oncidium with a principal role in hybrid production with odontoglossums and which grows in strong, bright light. These characteristics are subdued to the odontoglossum species requirement for coolness and moisture.

Air flow, although associated with cooling, is also necessary at times for warmth, as the conglomerate plants dislike low temperature in the daytime for an extended period. Although the functions of air flow and warmth supply may be combined in one unit, it is better done by using separate units, either of which can be cut out through relays and thermostats. Temperature control starts at bench level once shading has given every advantage that can be obtained from it.

Dry benching suitable for epiphytes like cattleyas or dendrobiums has little to offer specialist growers of odontoglossums who are interested in better cultivation and flowers. Quality lies not only in the number of flowers on a raceme but equally in the substance of flowers and the density of colour.

Odontoglossums should be grown on wet benches, and either of two systems may be tried. The first is to use terracotta pots in direct contact with a bed of damp to wet gravel about 4 to 5 centimetres deep (about 2 inches). The other method uses the same wet gravel bed, with plastic pots raised on mesh or in some other way to about 4 or 5 centimetres above the bed. Either system is effective in delivering a totally moist atmosphere about the plants, with the moisture renewed in the gravel every day if necessary up to saturation point. The system illustrated in micro-climates is also ideal for masdevallias.

Odontoglossums are cultivated as terrestrial orchids—they are grown in pots and the roots are principally contained in those pots. But the resemblance to the majority of the pseudo-terrestrial orchids with bulbs ends there, because at no time during the year should the potting material dehydrate.

An extract from the *Gardeners' Chronicle* of 9 September 1899 has as much impact almost a century later as it had on the readers of the time who grew odontoglossums:

The excellent remarks by Mr W. H. Young on page 188 of last week's issue of The Gardeners' Chronicle induce me to describe my own method of treatment and the course of reasoning which led to its adoption. In the first place, as this plant grows at an altitude of 8000 feet it must always be in free air and as the vapour-laden clouds rise to that height they become condensed and descend in copious showers upon the plants frequently but not constantly, and not at any time can the showers become warm. One could not imagine such a thing as a spike of bloom becoming spotted and disfigured, as one has often seen them in cool orchid houses.

As I grew my own plants and had not to please another's fancy, a bold method was adopted with marked success.

The essential points are: air is always admitted (except in a wind-frost) and especially by low ventilators opposite the hot-water pipes, with sufficient top ventilation to keep the air in the house in movement.

What I am now about to mention will no doubt raise a chorus of surprise and dissent. All the watering the plants get is from the cold hose-pipe once or twice a day to imitate the cold showers they get in their native habitat. This is given overhead as if they were so many cabbages. If the sheaths at the base of the pseudo-bulbs are full of water they are left so, the free ventilation puts that matter right and the material in the pots is never soaking wet, as though we were attempting to grow bog-plants. It is remembered that Odontoglossums grow on trees and can only get such water as falls from above. Keep the ventilation free—not so free as in an orchard-house, of course. But be bold and all will be well. Do not coddle your plants as regards temperature, but keep it down to 60 degrees in the summer if you can; and should it fall to 35 degrees on a winter morning do not faint with fright—your plants will not die if all other conditions have proper attention.—T.L.C.

Perhaps the signature tells it all.

This cold water treatment for odontoglossums has been part of my program ever since I started growing them so many years ago.

The root systems of odontoglossums, which despite the inclusion of other genera in the parentage are almost always fine, measure on average about 1 to 2 millimetres (about 1/32 to 1/16 of an inch). They may be damaged through overwatering, but damage is usually caused by poor potting technique and not because they are constantly moist.

Use of the correct amount and type of drainage material and correct elimination of excess water through its base have as much to do with successful cultivation of the genus as any other factors. The TLC should start with the purchase of the first plants.

Since odontoglossums need constant moisture, they should be benched on wet gravel regardless of external weather conditions. The system offers a model for the genus and every necessary feature is included. Cultivation techniques must be developed from this model, beginning with an understanding of odontoglossum plant development. In a fashion similar to nearly all orchids with or without pseudo-bulbs, the plants should increase in size by producing multiple new growths until the surface of the container is almost totally covered and the interior cannot support further root development.

In optimum culture the roots will usually take up all available pot space fairly quickly, before the surface is covered. If plant multiplication factors are good and there are more than single pseudo-bulb additions annually the containers will become too small in a matter of two to three years. There is no fixed rule for repotting, because propagations of different clones have unequal growth rates. The variation may be even greater when the same clone is grown and propagated by growers in different regions.

Your prime aim should be to retain foliage for as long as possible and quickly to discover the reason for any abnormal leaf losses. It may be a matter of incorrect environment or inappropriate cultural techniques. It may occur from root loss, although odontoglossums are not prone to fail in this regard as much as other genera.

Loss of leaf tips or partial failure of the leaf system is frequently held to be the result of high temperature, but may be caused by the environment or by plants becoming too dry at the roots. Often this is hard to detect until the foliage shows signs of stress. Affected plants should be examined, and if lack of moisture is the cause they should be stood in a dish of water for a couple of hours and then watered thoroughly from the top. After a day or so they should be again soaked and then rebenched with the rest of the collection. If the same plant is again affected, the potting material may be too loose or have another defect.

Sometimes light intensity is to blame, but the indicators for this are usually reddening of the leaves and a dry-looking surface. Ribbing or slight shrivelling appears to be common to the genus when flowering, and this also reflects on culture rather than any other cause. It is not a good sign but has no serious consequences unless it persists.

Repotting at the wrong time or harsh handling may also affect pseudo-bulbs and cause shrivelling, but if the environment is good and the potting material moist and vital this is corrected as soon as new roots begin to penetrate the potting material.

Natural leaf loss is common to the genus at certain times in the annual cycle, with no uniformity among the plants. It usually happens as flower spikes are growing and the strength of the plants is concentrated in that activity. The first to fail should be the short enclosing leafy sheaths at the base of the pseudo-bulbs.

If plants are healthy a flower spike should open almost continuously from buds which are little different in size from top to

bottom. There is something wrong with the program if the buds at the head of the spike are small and undeveloped when the lower buds are opening. A healthy plant will also carry the flower spike with no loss of condition for a matter of a few weeks; but the longer the flowers are left on the plants, the more delay occurs in formation of new growths. They have no real flowering program as far as seasons are concerned, but flowers produced in warmer periods of the year are seldom as good as those of late autumn, winter and spring.

Propagation should be considered immediately the flowers have been removed and before the foliage on older bulbs is discarded. There is only about half as much chance of further propagating clones if pieces are removed at repotting. Divisions should be made and the plant or plants left intact for at least another year.

If repotting is delayed, it is almost impossible for odontoglossums to grow more than about four pseudo-bulbs before they show signs of debility. For this reason, propagation should not be put off for the sake of possible flowering on better growths. The practice of dividing plants while they look strong is good programming and any second thoughts about it should be dismissed.

Leafless pseudo-bulbs seldom produce shoots, because the loss of leaf usually indicates that there are no viable eyes and roots on that portion.

The year after division of the rhizome, when repotting, you may notice that a small shoot has been formed on the severed bulbs, and that this new growth has no roots. In this instance the small propagation should be put in a small pot with a pad of sphagnum moss under the base and it will quickly produce roots; these should be given about three weeks to set, and then the propagation potted. Keep pests at bay while it is vulnerable.

A thin, very sharp knife should be used to make propagating incisions in rhizomes of odontoglossums. Such a knife is easily made from an old hacksaw blade ground to a taper and then given an edge, which need not be honed, as it is all the better when rough. Flame-sterilise it before each cut is made.

The leading or newer parts severed on plants should consist of no fewer than two mature pseudo-bulbs plus leads or new growths. There is no reason to suppose that the leads will not flower or will be weakened by removal of older and slowly dying parts of plants. By the time new growths have matured, made new root systems and flowered, the older parts which were severed should have new shoots, although perhaps still immature.

A hazardous propagation is severance of only a single new pseudo-bulb and its lead or new growth. This form of propagating

PROPAGATION OF THE WHOLE PLANT

Every plant in specialist collections of whatever genus should be subject to propagating techniques which have two aims in view: to increase the number of flowering growths and to induce parts of plants which are wasting to produce new growths and thus add to the number of divisions available from worthwhile clones.

The principle is to leave the newest parts of plants intact with sufficient backup material to ensure that they will not suffer in any way.

If for any reason plants cast leaves too soon, these non-working parts in most instances lose the capacity to produce new shoots from the normally operative eyes. The lifespan of leaves varies from genus to genus, but a good average is three to four years on cultivated plants, and longer on naturally growing plants. By severing older parts of plants before the leaves have lost their capacity, their vigour is retained, although it does not match that of the strong forward parts.

The lower picture illustrates the correct pattern for plants to follow: the plant is producing two new growths instead of only one from the leading or forward pseudo-bulbs.

If for any reason plants fail to carry out this natural increase it should

be taken as an indication that the environment is lacking some factor. It could also be a reflection on the grower for perhaps having selected a badly suited plant.

This propagation was the beginning of the specimen plant of *Lycaste* Shoalhaven illustrated on page 76.

important to have at least one of the bulbs carrying a leaf or leaves. It will be noted that the severed pseudo-bulb is still carrying the leaf, which indicates that when severed the portion had live roots and still does. Most leafless pseudo-bulbs do not have live root remaining; if there is a small remnant still alive it will die when disturbed.

The plant has been removed from the pot which it had occupied for perhaps three years. The potting material is still fresh and not soggy. In repotting the two portions the same type and proportions of potting material will be used.

The main part of the plant shows new growth at a well-leafed stage and this indicated, before the plant was removed from the pot, that it would have new roots at its base to add to plant support. This proved to be correct.

In handling other genera where there has been no division but plants have the same indications from the appearance of new growths, enough potting material should be scraped away or removed from the surface so that the base of the new growth is revealed, as in the lower picture.

The state of these new roots indicates that the plant may be repotted if thought necessary, being careful in handling that the new roots are not damaged.

CORRECT TIMING FOR REPOTTING

The advantages of plant division are well illustrated in the specimen above from a genus or conglomerate group termed odontoglossums, which do not readily or regularly produce double leads from the front parts of plants.

In the year before the plant was obviously ready for repotting, the rear part was severed carefully from the main plant structure between two pseudo-bulbs. In this genus it is weakens the plant structure, and any flower spikes which appear should be removed as soon as noticed. But occasionally this is the only way a propagation can be forced. If you must do it, you should inspect the plant regularly by digging gently around the roots to see when the older part produces a growth with roots. This is the signal to divide and repot the propagation from the main portion. This sort of propagation should be done only if it is wiser to have two sections of a doubtful plant rather than having all one's eggs in one basket. The whole thing must be handled carefully as there is risk of losing everything.

In propagating by severance, the two portions should be gently forced apart with the flat of the knife and some fungicide or a mixture of lime and fungicide drifted into the cut surfaces. A 50 per cent mix of the two is a reliable form of treatment.

Yellowing of odontoglossum foliage should be taken seriously if it appears on stronger portions of plants which have recently been severed. Where possible plants should be removed from containers and the root systems cleaned completely of old material and trimmed back until only good root is left. At the same time, examine the rhizome and pseudo-bulbs closely for signs of softness. Remove any infected parts and put the remnant or remnants into small pots containing a few strands of sphagnum moss and hope for the best. This is the only time when propagations should be repotted immediately after severance.

Emphasis is frequently put on the part which temperature plays in the cultivation of odontoglossums. While these orchids are plants of cool to temperate climates, they will grow in daytime temperatures which may at times reach 42 degrees Celsius (about 105 degrees Fahrenheit). They do so in my glasshouse, provided the night temperature can be reduced to about 15 to 20 degrees Celsius (about 60 to 70 degrees Fahrenheit). It should be understood, however, that these are only occasional highs and not regular summer happenings.

The principal test I have always applied is that sphagnum moss should grow freely and well on the same bench as the plants, and also on the surface of the potting material. Pure-bred odontoglossum species may be different, but as there are so few of them cultivated it is scarcely worth while planning for them. In years past I grew plants of *Odontoglossum crispum* (Lindley) with inter-generic hybrids quite successfully, and I found that the moss test for a growing environment always held good.

It could be asked whether heat affects flowering. Heat certainly affects the quality of flowers and it is an unfortunate characteristic of the hybrid conglomerate that many of them flower in late summer and early autumn. As a genus they flower when it suits plant development. While a clone may flower in late summer one year it may flower in autumn or winter in the next year.

In specialising it is possible to influence flowering periods to some extent. This may be done by various means which should be determined as part of a process by individual growers. But it should be realised that these orchids cannot be seasonally controlled like carnations or chrysanthemums, which can be induced to flower—within reason—when it suits producers.

It is possible to buy clones, sometimes rather expensive, which are fairly punctual, but if odontoglossums are particularly wanted for a certain season with dependability, say, for showing, then two or even three plants of such clones should be grown. This is when their extreme flowering variability becomes obvious.

8 BUILDING A QUALITY COLLECTION

Anyone who has created a specialist collection of any genus will agree that it is a difficult thing to start; it is even more difficult to cull from time to time and to fill the gaps with improvements in the standard. The criterion need not necessarily be shape or symmetry of flowers; it could as easily be colour.

The beginning of such collections could be through single plants which prospered in mixed groups of orchids, perhaps indicating to growers that the genus was worth an increase in numbers because it seemed to be suited by the environment.

Success with a particular plant, whether by chance or design, may persuade you to increase a section of your pastime into specialist culture. Each genus needs its own environment and whether it is the odontoglossum in a cool climate or phalaenopsis or vandas in warmer regions the best thing to do is follow the indicators.

Since we have mentioned odontoglossum, we may take it a little further and use the inter-bred complex as an example of creation of a specialist type of collection. For any other genus, all that has to be done is modify the requirements to suit, *always considering the prevailing climate in the region.*

In the 1980s in Australia, particularly southern Australia, the odontoglossum complex was popularised by production of hundreds of flasks of seedlings. This was a project of the Australian Orchid Foundation to finance the many tasks they set themselves. Each flask contained some twenty to thirty seedlings, comprising viable plants, with about an equal number of undeveloped plants and protocorms.

In some instances, no doubt, purchasers obtained very poor results because their environment was wrong and caused almost total loss. For others the reverse prevailed and if all the seedlings had grown there would scarcely have been room for them, let alone other orchids. These flasks of seedlings introduced odontoglossums to growers who otherwise would not have gone to the trouble of importing and quarantining them.

Flasks of seedlings are the source stock of many genera, and careful removal of the plants from the flasks and correct treatment thereafter is essential in building collections. The treatment from flask to flowering plants needs understanding and patience.

Some genera are difficult, but as this is about odontoglossums we may temporarily disregard the others and offer the idea of similar treatment for them.

The seedlings may be removed from flasks when ready by grasping those with developed leaves carefully with a pair of long tweezers and gently pulling the roots from the jell in which they have grown. Occasionally there may be a tangle with other small plants, particularly with the curled root systems which they are prone to develop. Using the other hand—if you have three, which seems a necessity at times—try working the plantlets apart with a thick plastic knitting needle.

The alternative is to break the flask. Wrap it in two or three sheets of newspaper and give it a sharp rap with a small hammer or similar medium heavy instrument. Sometimes flasks are difficult to break. Sort out the seedlings from the broken glass and the jell, removing as much of the wet material as possible from the base of the plants. They may be washed if necessary in clean water, but do not add any fungicide or other chemicals to the water.

The contents of flasks should be sorted into sizes. Plant the strongest in loose beds of growing sphagnum moss in shallow containers, such as ice-cream trays. Do not use old, brown or dry moss. The trays should be put into plastic bags, the necks tied with twist ties or rubber bands and placed in light of medium intensity. Alternatively the bags could be suspended in a shady but warm section of the growing enclosure or glasshouse, or even in a sunroom with good light. Do not expose the plants to direct sunlight until they are stronger.

Seedlings should be left in the bags until they start to make new roots, which may take as short a time as three weeks or as long as three months. The plantlets should not be watered, because there is enough residual moisture in the moss to keep them in good condition. Do not let the moss dry out, and remove the trays periodically to examine the contents.

Other methods may be more suitable for this primary treatment of seedlings, but in every instance the thoroughness and care with which the process is carried out will increase the number of survivors and their progress. The system is applicable to any genus but it may need some modification for tropical regions or colder climates or if seedlings are removed in colder months of the year. Deflasking should be timed to suit the genus concerned and its period of annual growth. This is not always possible, and with odontoglossums especially it is very difficult to state which is their period of dormancy or growth. The first experience may not be successfully carried out, but should be analysed and corrections made. Seek advice where possible.

The old roots which were formed in the flasks are mostly useless, and generally serve only to hold the small plants in place. Once new roots appear the small plants should be potted in small containers, plastic or terracotta, in a finer sample of the material used to grow the adult plants. If you are unused to handling the genus, put the plants into terracotta pots in fine fir bark for preference or an aggregate as fine as sugar and up to the size of peas. This should be kept continuously damp, preferably environmentally. Do not water the plants by spraying over the foliage. If possible keep it dry.

These points apply to nearly all flask-grown plantlets; they depend on associated humidity to maintain their condition. If infections or fungi affect the plants, use sprays very carefully and in weakest of concentrations. Survival depends on care and attention to detail, but there are sure to be natural casualties of morphologically weak plants in most flasks. It happens in all genera.

If all goes well, root growth and leaf growth will progress together, and within six to twelve months the first small pseudo-bulbs should have formed. From then on, if the environment is correct, the plants may be freely watered and should grow regardless of seasons. By the third pseudo-bulb they should show flower spikes, which appear usually within the largest of the leaves enclosing the pseudo-bulbs. The small plantlets may flower on their first or second pseudo-bulb if they are particularly strong and environmentally suited.

This process in any genus may take three or more years to fulfil, but by then your specialist collection should be well on the way. Within that period the temptation to obtain or buy plants in other than the specialist genus should be resisted, despite empty spaces on benches or in the enclosure. Efforts should have been made, however, to buy as many propagations within the genus as possible, preferably concentrating on clones which have quality or attractively coloured flowers. The illustrations show what is meant by quality and colour, and other odontoglossums are illustrated in *Growing Orchids, Book Two*.

Returning to the removal of plantlets from flasks, after treatment of those plants with strong leaves and growth, there are also numerous rubbishy smaller plantlets and almost leafless protocorms. Some of these, provided they do not look like conglomerate green masses, may in time grow and develop leaf and root shoots. (The conglomerate masses seldom thrive and grow unless they are cleaned and reflasked, which is a task beyond most growers.) The small undeveloped plantlets should be treated like the stronger ones: placed on damp growing sphagnum moss in shallow trays and similarly put into plastic bags. They should be given if possible slightly warmer conditions and a little less light than the developed plants. These undeveloped plantlets are troublesome and often frustrating, but if they finally grow they have been known in some instances to produce the best seedlings from cross-pollinations, in whatever genus. The temptation to discard them when deflasking should be resisted, although there is no certainty they will ever grow or be any good. Those which develop sufficiently should be treated in the same manner as the stronger plants and potted in similar material.

There is often some reward for using the topping of moss from some of the old strong plants in the collection as a top-dressing on the potting material of the seedlings, both the initial plantings of strong seedlings and also the later potting of the bits and pieces. The moss is probably impregnated with a valuable fungus aid to growth which is common to the root systems of strong adult plants in collections of many genera. If nothing is gained, certainly nothing is lost.

Another way of achieving the same result, whatever the genus being processed, is to remove a live root tip or two from adult plants of the genus. This should be crushed on a saucer and mixed with water which has been boiled and cooled. This should contain the relevant mycorrhizal fungus which assists growth and if the potting material used for the plantlets is moistened with it following planting the chances of growth and development are greatly increased.

Specialising in odontoglossums, or any genus, does not mean that a grower should have a collection of good names. It means essentially that growers should aim at producing fine plants. Because of this, specialists in species orchids of many genera—a rather uncommon group in any orchid-growing community—may never have much to show in ribbons and awards, but their plants and flowers will make up for it.

It is not easy to obtain propagations of exceptional clones. Buying flasks, raising seedlings and culling them after flowering is a satisfactory—if long and troublesome—way of building a specialist collection. It is one in which the author has had some experience. The experience went a little further than that, as it became apparent that so far as odontoglossums are concerned it is not as easy to discard them as it is cymbidiums or Slippers.

Occasionally flasks of mericlones are advertised, as well as adult meristem propagations of meritorious or colourful clones. A detrimental factor in relation to clonal propagations is the risk that they may be from second or third generation mericlone material. They are worth buying only if they are reasonably priced, or are purchased from originators of the clones in question. Reference to the illustrations of Blc. Malworth on page 109 may clarify that point.

Prices, of course, fluctuate from time to time, but the rule of supply and demand pertains in most instances. Occasionally prices for outstanding propagations may be fixed at what in normal conditions would appear outrageous levels, particularly if based on meristem propagations. However, it is fairly safe to say that no material from original clones will be released, and it may be years before the market is saturated to the point where such orchids become cheap or freely available.

In some countries a law is in force which prohibits buyers from disposing of propagations of certain registered plants. In some ways this law is completely unworkable, particularly where exchanges of plants occur between individuals.

Once it appears to a grower that a seedling is of outstanding merit, the propagating system illustrated and described should be put into operation and duplicates created. These duplicates should be exchanged, if necessary, for other meritorious clones to further enhance your collection. They should not be easily parted with, particularly to commercial propagators. Exchanges of mutually acceptable clones, perhaps not even in the same genus, are by far the most satisfactory ways of diversifying or adding to specialist collections.

If plants of outstanding quality are flowered the proposition of mericloning should be thought of. An expert propagator can be engaged to flask the meristems and such propagators advertise in most orchid journals. The anonymity of the clone should be preserved, so use a number or other indicator to identify the material in order to prevent unscrupulous use. It may be necessary to disclose the genus or genera involved but nothing should be offered beyond that. Possibly further information on this point should be sought from a trustworthy source. Make sure that the propagator understands how many flasks you need, and the stage to which they should be developed before you will take delivery.

Mericloning is a fairly long-term project which calls for patience.

If you wish to buy guaranteed top quality original propagations, there will probably be some releases at times. When they become available it is usually through advertisements in various orchid journals that the release is notified. There should be a verifying guarantee with these propagations, and purchasers through importation are obliged to take all the risks imposed by quarantine treatment.

Each genus offers its own particular problems in forming groups of some excellence, but if all the prerequisites of climate, environment and general planning are first assured, most of the problems can be resolved fairly easily.

9 GROWING METHODS

POTTING MATERIALS

Most potting mediums can be changed to suit a number of genera. The ideal is to make up those which need the least modification to suit both specialist genera and the compatibles which may be benched with them.

Every combination should be related to the environment in which it is used and consideration given to porosity, moisture-holding and every other factor. The analysis is easy for some growers, but for others the simple difference between plastic or terracotta pots and the need or not for crocking them becomes a matter for worry. Everyone has different approaches, but they all have to learn the same lessons. Some measure the quantities when mixing potting materials, which is the correct thing to do, while others make a rough guess, in which case no two combinations they make up are the same.

Dislike of particular constituents of potting mediums must be based on experience or knowledge and not simply be a matter of prejudice. For example, I have a personal dislike of charcoal because of an unfortunate experience, and I find myself advising against its use. Charcoal is a filler, simple and supposedly inert; its role is to act as a drainage medium and support the plant. The plants we grow in general derive little other than support from the materials we use, but the proportions must suit the growth patterns of those plants. Some materials are toxic or otherwise unacceptable to orchid roots and most of these are known. Charcoal could be toxic and if so, like other substances, it quickly puts an end to all root action; the plants lose stability and anchorage and the developed pseudo-bulbs if they have them, which are their storehouses, quickly deteriorate.

The specialist must beware of all these traps and preferably must not commit the collection to any medium which has even a possibility of undesirable characteristics.

If bark is used it should be the best procurable and in sizes or grades to suit the various genera. Odontoglossums should be thought of as epiphytes growing in terrestrial compounded potting mixes. The moderately fine roots should penetrate right through the potting mix and preferably be visible through the drainage holes, if they do not actually extend beyond them. If they do not do so there is something wrong with either the environment or the potting mix, probably the latter. Other genera should also follow this pattern.

Some thought should be given to the relative quantities of the components and their size. Each mix should be matched to the environment in which the plants are grown and it may take a little time to get it right. Sorting out the deficiencies and correcting them by means of trial and error is the only path to specialist success. If root systems indicate failure, some modification is called for and consultation with an orchid-growing friend is often helpful. Watch for impermeable bark and potting mixes which are too tight.

Several grades and several types of bark are commonly available. It may be found that imported bark gives a better result, but local products should be tried. A reason for selecting imported bark could be its better water absorption qualities, which is very important in potting material of any sort. It should be absorptive but not prone to go sour. Very little work on this aspect has been done.

Pot size determines to a degree the type and average size of potting materials. It is possible to state a good average size to suit most fine-rooted genera which are grown as terrestrial orchids. This results when all the materials are put through a 10-millimetre mesh, which is about three-eighths of an inch. Once the coarse aggregate has been sieved out for use with cattleyas and other coarse-rooted epiphytes, the bark and any other inclusions should be sieved to remove anything smaller than 2 to 3 millimetres. This gives an aggregate potting material which suits most orchids up to pots of about 10 centimetres. The smaller aggregate with the dust sieved out is ideal for seedlings or small propagations. For larger sized plants a small amount of coarser bark is returned to the mix and this forms a suitable combination for pots up to 125 milli-metres. Anything larger than that would need more readjustment.

There is no reason why with a well-adjusted fertiliser program such mixes comprising equal parts of bark and drainage material should not prove efficient and adequate. Drainage additives such as scoria, charcoal, gravel or stone should be thoroughly washed

The type of root system should dictate the nature of potting material and the method to be used. Coarse roots, such as those of this zygopetalum, should have fine aggregate material blended with coarse and preferably include some organic matter, such as peanut shells, rice hulls, or part decayed oak leaf. The roots are coarse, like those of cymbidiums and a successful mix for that genus should suit all orchids with such systems. The roots should preferably be covered, although it is not essential.

before use, principally to get rid of contaminants. The combination of the two should not vary beyond one part of drainage material to three parts of bark or one part of drainage material to two parts of bark, which are rather stony mixes. The final settlement on a stable mix should be made over a period of about three years and preferably using divisions of one clone for trial plants. This is also applicable to other genera, whatever potting materials are used.

When potting, make sure that the drainage component does not separate out as it is inclined to do. Turning the mix over frequently prevents this. The mix should be thoroughly damp yet not wet. It should flow into the root systems and not have to be forced into containers. Make sure that there are no air pockets left in containers. These tend to dry plants out and reduce water or moisture retention.

For odontoglossums I have suggested using terracotta pots benched on wet gravel or bench filling, and plastic pots on staging above it (see page 142). Odontoglossums thrive in almost saturated bench conditions in terracotta pots and I have always found that in all phases of growing, flowering or inactive stages the plants and root systems proliferate better when a thin layer of growing sphagnum moss is cultivated on the surface of the potting material. It turns pale when the plants are too dry or underwatered and is a valuable indicator of the condition of the potting material. However, it may not suit all environments.

As I do not use or advocate use of plastic pots for odontoglossum culture it is not possible for me to state that the moss growth is beneficial or harmful when using them. For what it is worth, my opinion is that contrary to indicating the state of the potting material in plastic pots it could give a false reading.

This should not be taken to mean that plastic pot cultivation is any less successful than terracotta pots, but it is most unwise to mix the two. A completely different environment and growing pattern must be worked out for each, right down to modification of the proportion of drainage to bark material. It still remains a stable recommendation that the quality in each instance should be the same, with a preference for good-quality bark and clean, inert drainage material.

For epiphytes such as dendrobiums there is a choice of materials, but the desirable feature is openness and free drainage of excess water. The filling (because that is virtually all it is) for any container should be acceptable to the roots. If on contact they brown off, or cease activity when they should be proliferating, the potting mix should be discarded immediately and a fresh start made with another blend. The nutrient program should also be examined to see if any ingredient was unacceptable. In good culture the root system should move to the sides of containers and cling there, although at times certain inclusions in the mix will attract roots and hold them.

All epiphytes should be encouraged to grow and remain in containers for a number of years, with the aim to produce maximum effect in flower. This is achieved only when a plant is able to reach a mature size, holding as much of its foliage as possible and retaining a virile working root system.

Hard materials like scoria or stone have been used for a long time for epiphytes. It has not always proved successful, but a certain amount of innovation has been achieved by growers in all climates. Stone—and scoria is included in the use of the word—depends for success on an understanding of methods and genera which will tolerate it. It is also necessary to understand the difference between it and the bark and charcoal mixes commonly used.

This plant is growing in coarse, smooth, water-washed river pebbles and has been in the container for a number of years, each growth showing improvement. When using bark and charcoal or other drainage material a steady deterioration occurs, rendering it unusable in further potting. This does not apply to stone, which can be washed and used over and over again. However, it may not be suitable for all epiphytic orchids.

Here and there amongst the stones small pieces of moss should be used, preferably sphagnum moss, which is long lasting. This serves as a reservoir of moisture in an otherwise very dry medium. The roots will penetrate to the bottom of containers where there would probably be a small residue of water and because of effective aeration through the slits

in the lower side of pots such as this the roots will remain virile and not decay.

The nature of the finer gravel is clear in the lower picture and this can be used for small plants and seedlings. It is smooth and does not compact to retain moisture, but it also would be improved by inclusion of small tufts of sphagnum moss as the containers are filled. All sand and dust should be washed and sieved out of the pebbles.

Epidendrum cinnabarinum
(Salzm.). One of the reed-
stemmed group in this
large genus, possibly the
largest of the kind usually
designated Crucifix
Orchids. It is Brazilian,
where it is widespread,
also common to other
South American states,
principally best considered
as an orchid for
intermediate temperatures.

Encyclia brassavolae
(Reichenbach f.). One of
the most beautiful of the
Mexican encyclias, from a
fairly high altitude of
about 1000 to 1800 metres.
However, it is not a cold-
growing species and would
fail to flower if grown that
way. It may also be a risk
subject for the tropics, but
if there is any tolerance at
all it would be toward that
type of climate. It is
affiliated to *E.
prismatocarpum* or
prismatocarpa
(Reichenbach f.),
depending on which book
is consulted.

Epidendrum Elfin
(*Epi. cochleatum* x *Epi. prismatocarpum*). This beautiful orchid was bred from a Mexican orchid now known as *Encyclia cochleata* (Linnaeus), which was transferred by Lemee in 1955, and the Central American species *Epidendrum prismatocarpum* (Reichenbach f.). Both these orchids are most attractive and their better features come to the fore in the hybrid.

In recent years, looking at taxonomy in the 1980 decade, many of the epidendrums were transferred to other classifications. The name encyclia was originally given to the genus by Hooker in 1828, seventy-five years after Linnaeus created the genus epidendrum, a name which covered many of the orchids known at that time, including cattleyas.

The distinction between the two genera is principally founded on the fact that most of the epidendrums have a reed-like monopodial growth while the recognisable characteristic of encyclias is that they have pseudo-bulbs. Thus *Epidendrum* Elfin should be known as an encyclia because it has pseudo-bulbs. But here, as in many other examples, the fact that it was registered and listed in Sander's List of Orchid Hybrids as an epidendrum probably consigns it to that category for all time.

Encyclia cochliata (Linnaeus) closely resembles *Epidendrum* Elfin, although we perhaps should express the relationship in the reverse way. It flowers in spring, although the pseudo-bulbs commence to grow from the base of the older ones almost as soon as the flowers fade.

Most of the epiden- drums and encyclias will not grow in cool to cold conditions and could be classed as intermediate climate orchids. The tolerance of these intermediate climate orchids generally extends into the warmer levels but there is little scope for quality flowers in the wrong environment.

166

Epidendrum pseudo-wallissii. One of the most beautiful of the genus but about which there is little information and it is not commonly known among orchid growers. *E. wallissii* (Reichenbach f.) is a very similar but more heavily marked orchid from Colombia which is also little known or grown.
It is a reed-stem type, first described by Reichenbach in 1875 and the two are possibly conspecific.
It should grow in the sub-tropics and perhaps doubtfully in tropical climates.

Encyclia vitellinum (Lindley). One of the most difficult of the genus to grow, this Mexican orchid from about 2000 to 3000 metres has been in cultivation for more than 150 years. It is cool-growing and very demanding on a special environment. The distinguishing morphology for encyclias is that in general they have recognisable pseudo-bulbs.

Epidendrum stenopetalum (Hooker). A reed-stemmed epidendrum with rather thickened pseudo-bulbs compared with *E. ibaguense* and others. It is most beautiful, common to much of Central America also more rarely South America, and is a tropical, almost sea-level, plant in Venezuela.

Comparettia macroplectron (Reichenbach and Triana). An epiphyte from intermediate climate which has proved very difficult to carry through many years of cultivation. Such orchids are individual projects worth studying. The beautiful panicles of flower carried on this orchid are worth all the trouble. It has rather small pseudo-bulbs, fairly large leaves, would grow best on sections of branches in open-rooted fashion and treefern slabs could prove unsuitable.

Neolehmannia peperomia (Reichenbach f.), syn. *N. porpax* or *Epidendrum porpax*. A most beautiful miniature from Brazil with a tufted habit producing many new growths each year on correctly grown plants. It is moist-growing, seldom dormant, intolerant of dryness and unsuitable for warm conditions.

Sophronitella violacea (Lindley) Schlechter. Another miniature from Brazil, related to sophronitis, cool-growing and preferring open-rooted culture. It multiplies rapidly, producing two or more flowers on short stems from the apex of the pseudo-bulbs. The flowers open in midwinter and soon afterwards new growth appears, but moisture should be applied sparingly until new roots appear in summer.

168

Each genus or its associated hybrids, of course, require different circumstances and considerations. Climate will also dictate the use of different potting mixes. In high rainfall areas and cultivation in almost open conditions under Sarlon or synthetic fabric roofing, quite different procedures and potting materials should be used.

In some tropical areas the use of scoria has been general for a long time, but even with this medium several unacceptable fungi and algae find this a good propagating bed for their own purposes. The same agents cause bark mixes to break down too fast to make them even partly successful. However, bark may be an additive.

The disadvantages may be reduced to some extent by the type of structure in which the orchids are grown, but they are hard to eliminate completely. Some advantage is gained by using scoria for the lower two-thirds of a pot and filling the top portion of it with crushed rock. In this way the slightly porous scoria attracts and holds some moisture, while the upper rocky surface dries out very soon after watering. The root systems of such genera as cattleyas go to the moisture reservoir below the crushed rock and proliferate well in that zone, leaving the upper surfaces almost free of root growth. This is a very efficient way of overcoming the growth of fungi and algae because the surface is too dry for them, and they do not infest the scoria or moisture-retaining material because they must have light to survive. Whether it would be possible to include fir or pine bark in the lower portions of such mixes would be at the discretion of a grower and following a thorough trial on an inexpensive series of plants.

Stone or rock culture should not be confined to warmer or high rainfall areas. It is a very good system for some epiphytes, including the very large group of Australian dendrobium species and hybrids. Whatever stone is used—washed, rounded river pebbles are best— should be graded to suit pot size rather than root thickness. Root systems when orthodox mixes are used tend to go only half-way to the base of containers and then seal off or perhaps decay at the tips because of high moisture content on an essentially open-root plant. Stone culture encourages them to go completely to the base of containers and proliferate there if drainage and aeration of pots is good. This applies equally well in tropical cattleya culture.

One point in relation to fungi and algae should be made concerning tropical cultivation under shade-cloth. At least twice a year the shade-cloth should be sprayed on the upper surface with a fungicide to kill the spores which collect there. The effect is even better if rain follows such a spraying, because some fungicide will be washed down on the plants, where it helps to prevent the fungal infections and decay so common in humid climates. Corrugated plastic roofing should also be sprayed on the underside at least once a year. It may be entirely unnecessary, but it is good insurance against falling fungal spores. These will grow quite readily on the underside of both glass and plastic where there is the slightest amount of condensation.

The infection originating on shade-cloth is often responsible for unwanted surface growth of algae and fungi in ordinary soft potting materials. However, there is good reason to include small amounts of moisture-holding material, like moss, in the lower strata of stone culture. Such material may be compressed pellets of peat moss or of composted vegetable material like grass clippings. The pellets should be no bigger than an almond. Such inclusions should never be a major portion of the total and preferably only about 5 to 10 per cent. Strands of sphagnum moss may also be used in the stone topping and removed if seen to be hosting algae or fungi. Normally sphagnum moss is sterile and remains so.

EPIPHYTE CULTURE

As many as half the orchids grown for pleasure are quite unsuited by pot culture; they are epiphytes. It is almost impossible to duplicate the type of growth these plants produce in their habitats, and their life span in cultivation is probably considerably less than it would be if they were growing naturally.

To offset the disadvantages to plants, several innovations have been thought up over the 200-odd years of cultivation. Special terracotta pots have been designed and at times patented. The older literature is well illustrated with woodcuts and line drawings of the various forms this cultivation reached. The methods may have appeared strange, but usually little information was sent with the plants on their consignment from various parts of the world and only a few perceptive growers took the trouble to find out why the plants were dying as fast as they were unpacked. In the modern world some 200 years later the method of cultivation without pots or containers has developed from those first attempts to grow the plants as epiphytes.

The scientific appreciation of materials suitable for attachment of orchid roots is usually expressed as the relative acidity or pH of the materials. If further information about that is needed an encyclopaedia should satisfy the ordinary grower. We know a great deal about the relative merits of treefern slabs, sections of certain tree branches, sections of bark or cork (which again is simply bark),

which is vitally important to all epiphytes.

The lithophyte, such as the plant of *Dendrodium speciosum* (J. E. Smith) forms its food trap by proliferating a vertical root system to catch leaves and forest rubbish.

Each of these plants must be provided for in a different way. The epiphyte is essentially what we should call an open-rooted orchid—it will not tolerate being grown in a container. It must be grown on a slab of treefern, wood, or a section of tree branch, so the root system can develop on the surface. This mount must be acceptable to the roots, and discarded if they will not cling to it and grow.

On the other hand, the plant with the vertical food trap will grow its roots into a suitable below-surface medium. In this instance the plant is growing in a log or blister cut off a tree; it is the plant illustrated in *Growing Orchids, Book Three* on page 138.

Every genus and individual species or hybrid must be sorted according to the form of cultivation it prefers. With some genera such as cattleyas a single cultivation method may be applied to all the plants, the only difference being in size of the pots or the grade of material. With other genera more individual treatments are required.

As each plant is brought into a collection it should be assessed for growth pattern, remembering that some genera are lithophytic or rupicolous, some are epiphytic, and others naturally grow in ways which cannot be duplicated in artificial cultivation.

The top illustration is of a typical epiphyte. It is growing naturally in the fork of a tree and has formed its own food trap,

The development of the sarcochilus root system is obvious after eight months of attachment to the bark slab. The use of this bark was not a casual choice, but rather the result of some 17 years experience of growing plants on the live trees themselves. Comparative growing with cattleyas in casuarina bark and fir bark has shown that the fir bark was better. But it is equally possible that fir bark used as slabs for growing things like sarcochilus may prove poorer than slabs of casuarina bark.

Experimental growing is the only way to tell and it will usually be found that what suits one genus is not always as good for another genus.

even down to the relative acceptability of stone and scoria. All these materials must be slightly acid, never alkaline, or the roots avoid them or brown off on contact with them. One experience should be enough to warn a grower against continuing to use anything which the plant has rejected. Sometimes exposure to air and rain can change the quality of these materials and make them more acceptable, but the ideal is to find one of them which suits your environment and climate. No amount of persuasion should be able to have that material discarded or replaced by another.

It should not be thought that a particular genus is committed to any set type of cultivation. For example, some maxillarias are quite well suited by pot culture, but others prefer to be treated as epiphytes. It is best to follow the preference of each species.

Some species could never be satisfactorily grown if hanging space was unavailable. Catasetums and cycnoches could be taken as examples. Both are better cultivated in what are called slat baskets. At bench level these plants would be exposed to risk of unneeded moisture in a dormant period as pronounced as occurs in any genus.

A part or complete lithophyte such as this plant of sarcochilus cannot be cultivated in the way it grew when collected from a boulder in a mountain gully. The next best thing is a slab of rough casuarina or similar bark and a pad of mossy fibre placed under the base of the plant, which is tied to the slab with nylon fishing line. The root system of the plant has been truncated and partly destroyed and must be regrown.

For a large number of epiphytes needing open-root culture a rough-barked section of branch such as this is ideal. It is casuarina, the same as the smoother barked section. Each has its uses. Other trees such as oak are equally suitable, but the prerequisite is that the bark must be fairly permanent and not likely to be shed from the wood of the section too readily. It will usually be found that green branches do not shed the bark as quickly as dry or dead branches, in which the shedding process has already begun. If such tree sections are unavailable, slabs of weathered hardwood, red pine, ordinary untreated pine and a number of non-resinous timbers are very good, including the extreme luxury of cedar.

A bark slab mounted oncidium. These orchids are principally epiphytic and they have a peculiarity—not confined to this genus—of an upward pattern of growth. Not all oncidiums have this habit.

The ascending habit must be accommodated in a way that allows for a double growth eye to develop in any one year, a branching habit which many orchids have. It must be given a chance to proliferate and slabs must be wide enough to allow this. The slab is also treated differently by standing it in a potful of growing medium such as common cymbidium mix, which allows the roots to go down into the medium if they find it attractive. It is a coarse-rooted oncidium with a reputation for doing this.

173

It is common practice in southern parts of Australia to grow dendrobiums in pots, principally because they are easier to move about. But in sub-tropical and tropical areas where so many of the genus are dormant for a long period they may be grown with open roots.

This particular plant grows an intense and prolific root system and is entirely unsuitable for pot culture. A slab mount has been chosen which gives scope for the roots to develop in both ways—as anchorage for the plant and to take advantage of a humid environment.

It has been mounted in the same fashion as the sarcochilus (see page 173), with a pad of fibre and moss under the base of the plant to hold a small amount of moisture. But it is surprising how little use the plant makes of this residual moisture. The root system grows away from it and proliferates in the air.

The lower illustration indicates the progress of the root system after a matter of months. It is virile and, despite the low average temperature in which the plant grew (about 6 to 12 degrees for some months), there is no sign of root dormancy. In pot culture, with the usual pattern of bench cultivation, dormant plants may be stifled by lack of air circulation about root systems such as this. By cultivating epiphytic orchids in this way more use is made of the available space and plants may be suspended at any convenient points in the enclosure, whether it is of glass or shade-cloth.

The material used in such slat baskets, which are very easily made, should be of a type which can be dried out and reconstituted as a moist acceptable material for roots to recommence activity. It may be necessary to have a removable surface which can be replaced when the time comes to wake them up into growth and flower. If and when plants show new growth, the material should not be replaced or moistened to any degree until this new growth shows root or the older ones are noted to have produced new tips. Many catasetums and cycnoches live on dead wood which is completely dehydrated in dormancy. *The signal to these plants is a seasonal change which may have nothing more than a rise in humidity to indicate that it has arrived.*

Methods of attaching epiphytes to their host mounts can be as varied as the mounts. Nylon fishing line appears to be among the better materials. The best way to use it is to make a loop, using a slip-knot; put the loop over the mount and the firmest part of the root system and the pad of fibre which should be used under the base of the plant. The slip-knot is pulled tight and then knotted with the short end and the long tail to keep the plant firm. The long tail is then wound around the mount and the rest of the root system until the plant is firmly attached and does not flop about. The long end is then brought again to the short end at the slip-knot and tied firmly. To tie nylon fishing line it is necessary to go through the first loop again and again until four twists have been taken about the main length of the line. If pulled tight this four-twist loop pulls tight and will not slip.

Not everyone has fishing line handy to tie plants, but it would be unusual if there was any lack of old hosiery about to do the same job. Old hosiery should be slit lengthwise into strips: these are more easily tied and just as durable as fishing line. If for any reason it is necessary to create a small bag about the roots of the plant being tied to the mount, it can be formed with a wider strip of the same material.

10 USE OF FERTILISERS

In a specialist collection, I would advise against adopting a plan where strong nutrient solutions are fed to plants at infrequent intervals. The use of weak nutrient fertiliser each time the plants are watered has much to recommend it because it more closely approaches the natural order of things.

This statement should be qualified where terrestrial cultivated orchids like paphiopedilums or cymbidiums are concerned. With these and similar genera a solid fertiliser incorporated in a potting mix will be available for growth and flowering without overloading the growing medium. It is with such genera also that slow-release fertiliser pellets have their uses. However, they are not suitable for epiphytic orchids, and their release of fertiliser could also be unsuitable for some of the terrestrial cultivated types. In general they have little part to play in cultivating specialist collections. This should not be taken as denigration of such fertilisers overall, but their use and effect should be thoroughly understood. They are an ideal way of fertilising house plants, ferns and for other special uses.

In growing orchids, drainage and fertiliser are inextricably bound together. The allowance for drainage in most pots is inadequate for orchids, regardless of whether they are plastic or terracotta. In the latter the manufacturers' allowance for drainage should be doubled by carefully enlarging the hole. Plastic pots are sometimes manufactured with holes in the bottom, sometimes with slits in the lower part of the sides; they should preferably have both, and the base of the pot should be slightly convex when looked at from the top.

Crocks should be a matter of thought. Some growers do not use them at all, relying on the porosity of the potting material to prevent accumulation of excess moisture in the base of the pot.

Even the best blended materials tend to fail in this area at times, but it seldom occurs if pots are correctly crocked with broken pot or tile shards. The blend of some potting materials—such as used, for example, with smaller genera like odontoglossums—may contain leaf elements; these, as they decay, tend to break down to mud if retained for longer than two or three years. The potting materials used with such genera are mostly rather fine and need correctly placed crocks to protect the root systems from moisture overloads.

Root loss in any group, whether of isolated plants or much of a collection, is caused more by poor drainage than any other factor. The damage is often made worse by retention of unwanted amounts of fertiliser. Once the roots cease activity the whole potting system is affected and, strange as it may appear, the nature of the potting material undergoes a change. Each specialist, in whatever genus, should become aware of what the liquid in the pots (whether water or water with added fertiliser) is supposed to be doing and what it really is doing.

In many of the collections of orchids in this bicentenary phase of the pastime, electronics and automation play large parts in annual culture. Nutrients can be fed to the plants at regular intervals through reticulation. While this takes away something from specialist culture, it saves a lot of time *provided every plant is covered and there are no blind spots in the system.* In such systems a certain amount of unwanted fertiliser is spread about and a number of plants get moisture when they are not in need of it. However, with moderation there is no real damage except to the odd plant. Although the operators of these systems do not usually see such failures of odd plants as breakdowns in culture, if they are competent they will remove those plants, note why the system has failed at that point and preferably use some manual control over the specialist part of a collection, whatever the genus.

In surveying the odontoglossum complex (which could be compounded from any of the odontoglossums, cochlioda, oncidiums, miltonias, aspasias and perhaps other genera) the principal feature is their irregularity. This is also repeated to a degree in the cattleya complex. In these complex groups it is not possible to have a completely automatic fertiliser and watering system because of extreme variability of plant phases. If reliance is put on such a system then a cultural breakdown must occur at some point and damage may follow.

Some attempts are being made to cultivate the groups in unlikely climatic areas. Although it is possible to get flowers, their quality and lasting capacity are so poor that a change should be made to more suitable genera. The production of flowers is not always the yardstick by which to judge competence. Enterprise in this direction, however, is taking over in some ways and a new race of odontoglossum hybrids is probably on the way which will flower in quite warm climates, provided advantage is taken of the micro-climates present in most growing areas outside completely tropical regions.

In using fertilisers, the most constant sequence or patterns of growth should be considered without having any regard for variables such as those genera which never stop growing or flowering. The appearance of new growth usually signals capability to absorb moisture and accompanying nutrient liquid through the root system. But there should be no rush to saturate the plants; a gradual approach is needed. The environment should be first to take

The application of fertiliser to suspended plants can be a problem unless tackled in such a fashion. Equipment for this sort of fertilising is freely available and in sizes which can cope with large collections. It is also much simpler if one has grandchildren who need no encouragement and could possibly be the future generations of orchid growers. If this method is used for pesticides, protective equipment should be worn, including a face mask.

additional moisture; plants need only the secondary effect of atmospheric moisture to sustain them in preparatory stages of growth. Root systems are not necessarily brought into action immediately and there may be a gap of some weeks between appearance of growth and root activity. Where possible the base of new growth should be watched for root sprouts and these should be allowed to develop for a week or more before thorough periodic watering and fertilising commences.

Some genera, for example laelias, may fail to produce new root tips from new growth; instead they may initiate new tips on older roots and grow these for perhaps twelve months before new root is apparent on those new growths. In such instances it may be difficult to tell if the older roots are sprouting, but sufficient potting material should be carefully removed, if possible, to get a look at what the plants are doing.

Pest control is more important than fertilisers in the primary stage of root production, because it may be found that immature roots are incapable of producing new tips if they are eaten off by pests.

The period of maximum use by orchid plants of the fertiliser or nutrient solution is when new growth is apparently nearing maturity. At this stage the size of new growths may be increased by as much as 33 per cent by correct use of nutrients. At this stage also the number of flowers and their quality is determined. Once absolute maturity is reached a tapering off process should be commenced and applications reduced so that plants are maintained rather than forced.

The ultimate perfection of flowers rests with the total environment between the formation of spikes, racemes or stems of flowers and their opening. The substance or quality has been predetermined by the thoroughness of culture between appearance of new growth and primary flower development. Consideration of the prevailing climate is perhaps the most important feature in production of flowers.

The environment, including the fertiliser regime, must as far as possible match the requirements of all the plants grown, but never at the expense of the main genus. If that happens to be cattleyas the mixture may include laelias, both species and hybrid, and many other orchids and they must all be able to acclimatise to a constant fertiliser.

In general the fertilisers which these plants get when growing naturally are available all the time for the plants to pick up; there is no break in the supply unless a dry period intervenes in their annual cycle. There is no scope for arranging that in artificial cultivation, so the next best thing must be done, that is, reducing the fertiliser concentration to the degree where it is innocuous.

Some inequities must occur in any total fertiliser program and this is where the hard decisions must be made. All the weak plants must be eliminated slowly as they decline to accept the program, regardless of the nature or beauty of their flowers. The alternative is to make specialist growing even more specialist in character and isolate certain plants.

There will be other plants which ought to be eliminated: for instance those which appear to be structurally weak and after flowering go into a decline as though the effort is too much for them. There is no time for specialist growing which demands a couple of years spent reconstituting one or two plants. If an ordinary good environment and a constant program of weak fertiliser cannot sustain a plant then it is not fit to occupy space in a group of orchids assembled to fulfil above-average expectations.

The ideal, which of course is hard to attain, is for every plant in the collection to tolerate and use as necessary a weak form of fertilising nutrient throughout the year, perhaps with slight modification at some period or periods. The words as necessary are the test; the regime will not allow constant exceptions or consideration of the state of growth or flowering or dormancy of individual plants.

Such a program is possible. The movement of plants about the growing area might have to be part of it, but the general idea of top-quality flowering without forcing is the real answer to specialist aims.

Finally some consideration should be given to two of the warmest-growing orchids, phalaenopsis and vandas, best suited to those climates where temperatures, while uneven, do not fall to the levels usually associated with marked climatic differences between seasons.

Both genera, however conglomerate their form, are essentially open-rooted and obviously in growth or flowering. This pattern is not duplicated in colder climates, however the conditions may be modified to approximate the warmer cultural requirements, and the plants go into definite dormancy.

This is where the divergence in programming begins. On the one hand the plants grown in warmer climates are able to accept a program of constant fertiliser, but on the other hand any attempt at specialising must have regard to the state of various plants at any time through an annual cycle in cooler to cold climates.

This idea should be extended to any of the warm-growing genera in species or hybrid form. Although the vanda conglomerate is more heterogeneous than phalaenopsis, both have a fairly regular annual flowering cycle. Sometimes odd members fall out of step with the majority.

The basic reasoning is simplicity. The fertiliser itself should be simple in composition, without recourse to some of the more elaborate additives such as Formula 20, and it should always be made with measured quantities, much weaker than is usually recommended. The program of application should also be simple and regular. Like all aspects of orchid growing, the results depend on conscientious work with the orchids.

Tropical genera such as spathoglottis, calanthes and some of the epidendrums take very kindly to solid organic fertilisers which decay quickly. If these are applied in the form of topping on potting material they will offer nutrient each time the plants are watered. Within reason vandas in the conglomerate sense will also use such fertilisers and quickly locate and put roots into it. Most animal manures will decay quickly, but if fowl manure is used a great amount of care should be taken to avoid plant damage. There is some bias against fowl manure from some sources because of the antibiotics added to their feed.

Repetition can be tedious, but if growers, particularly specialists, realised how little fertiliser it takes to keep orchid plants in top condition many would modify the systems they are using. If a little thought is given to the origins of the plants and the manner of their growth the whole thing becomes obvious. For example, phalaenopsis growing naturally send out tremendous quantities of root in the search for food. The nutrients they seek are distributed in minute quantities on the surface of the trees or rocks they cling to, and only what is washed on to them by rain or other moisture can be absorbed.

In cultivation of these plants the root systems are frequently short and sparse by comparison and the food must be applied to them. Their need for nutrient is no greater. Food should be applied in minute quantities all the time as it is in nature; it should not be in quantities which are toxic and the best arrangement is to try to follow nature's pattern. Do not be afraid that they will starve—far from it. They will thrive.

There is some excuse for minutely increasing the strength of the fertiliser formula when plants are flowering, but it should be only a slight increase, not doubled or trebled.

The test for most orchids which flower on racemes, such as phalaenopsis, cymbidiums and odontoglossums, is for the buds to develop evenly in size for the total length of the spike and the first flowers to open about the middle of the raceme. If the lower buds open while the upper buds are only half-grown the environment is incorrect or the fertiliser is wrong and *the first thing to blame is the environment—not the fertiliser.* This test cannot be applied to all genera, especially such things as vandas which have a naturally consecutive method of developing flowers. The fertiliser system should remain the same, however, because in cultivation even these orchids with their rampant root systems do not produce them to the degree apparent in natural growing plants.

With fertiliser under control, retention of the correct amounts of moisture remains a consideration for terrestrial cultivated orchids. In this regard, many advantages are offered by the double-pot system, particularly in cultivating orchids like odontoglossums or Slippers, which prefer a wet bench.

The idea that plastic pots offer a moist-growing technique equal to the two-pot system could be put forward, but the theory does not work out in practice. It makes as much sense as the proposition that plastic pots are warmer than terracotta pots.

Briefly, the double-pot system uses a normal potting mix in clay pots which are then inserted into others which will fully contain them without being sloppy as already explained. In the bottom of the outer pots a few strands of sphagnum moss are used to make pads which serve two purposes—they remain wet or moist for some days and thus preserve a moist environment about the inner pots, and they also help to keep out the pests which penetrate into the pots through drainage slits or holes and so eat the roots which may be there.

The outer pots may be either plastic or clay. A little thought must convince a specialist of the protection this system offers to busy growers who may be away all day. In the hottest weather there would be confidence that the plants would have protection against dryness. Periodic dehydration and moistness is inadvisable for most terrestrial grown orchids. Terracotta pots breathe and if a little thought is given to that function it may be appreciated how well plants like odontoglossums would respond to that state where the inner pot remains moist, with similar effect for other such genera.

Where dormancy is required in some genera a little water may be trickled down between the two pots, which is the individual side of cultivation. If the outer pot is of terracotta, the moss pad may be moistened by dipping the base of the outside pot in shallow water, which is taken up by capillary action to reach the moss. There is no need to water such plants from the top because it would perhaps destroy the benefit of dormancy and affect the root systems.

There is no reason why the use of double pots could not be extended to most specialist genera with minor adjustments. If you use this system of culture there is no need to provide wet benches even for moisture-loving plants; plain mesh top or solid bare benching can be used. It may be expensive on pots, but after all they are perhaps the cheapest item in the pastime.

11 ORCHID ROOT SYSTEMS

TERRESTRIAL AND TERRESTRIAL-GROWN PLANTS

Root systems are the most misunderstood parts of orchid plants. There are three principal types—terrestrial, epiphytic, and aerial or open. Orchid roots are tough yet delicate systems, rejuvenated each year if they are properly cultivated, but totally destroyed if environments are wrong. Environment starts at the bottom of the pot and embraces everything else to the tips of the leaves and the atmosphere surrounding them.

It may appear trite to say that orchids grow where orchids grow, but this basic truth cannot be repeated too often. Every requisite life factor must be available in that position where each plant is to grow. In cultivation the roots should follow patterns which are similar to those of the orchid's original habitat; the illustrations in this chapter explain visually how growers, not necessarily specialists, should study each genus for the model which will encourage plants to reach their full potential.

It is possible to find several types of root systems within each genus, and there are enormous differences between genera. The root systems of paphiopedilums, which are totally hidden in most instances, are the direct opposite of the aerial systems of vandaceous plants. There is no way in which either genus could be accommodated in the potting system of the other, yet frequently they are included in the one environment. In this event the best that could be hoped for would be a median development in which neither the growth of the plants nor the flowers would reach their full potential. Consider how much more difficult it becomes when the project is a collection of species or hybrid orchids embracing several genera and inter-generic cross-pollinations. Orchid growers are guilty of this mal-practice throughout the cult or pastime, but it becomes less devastating on plants and less expensive and wasteful if information is sought and understanding gained about the habitat of any genus and the way its members grow.

In the course of years it is the common experience that some plants, despite every effort, fail to acclimatise, grow and flower. Primarily this could be caused by incorrect environment, an over-supply or deficiency of light, air, water or moisture, or poor tem-perature control. For any species there is always some information available about its habitats, the altitudes at which it grows, and the type of country—both geological formations and daily climate. Often one can find data on the periodic rainfall, orientation of the plants and associated ecological groupings.

For example, odontoglossums, that is some species used in producing what are today commonly referred to as odontoglossums, originated in the borders of rainforest on the mountains of Colombia, South America, at about 2000 to 3000 metres (about 6500 to 9600 feet above sea level). Although Colombia falls within the tropical region of South America, the height at which the orchids grow indicates that the climate would be almost cold. At this height also it would be moist to wet. A description of this climate was given in the *Orchid Review* in the early years of the twentieth century and when we compare some of the environments in which the genus is grown in the late years of the same century we can understand fully why the plants look so lifeless and give so little encouragement to growers to continue with them.

TERRESTRIAL ROOTS

Let us turn again to paphiopedilum or Slippers, as they are known, and the genera commonly grown as specialist groups. For com-parative purposes their root systems are best classified as terrestrial orchid roots. As with all orchids, the environment determines the nature and health of the root systems.

Although the roots are crammed into containers, each genus has morphological limitations which control the growth of the roots, their life span and their abandonment by plants as leaves are cast and new growth added. We become aware of this only when the roots are visible like those of vandas.

The orientation of plants could affect root growth if new vegetative growth travels toward a light source opposite to that which should be taken. The plants could be facing too much light or the opposite condition of too dense shade. The height of the bench or staging or on which side of an enclosure the plants are positioned could all affect growth and subsequent root development. It is not obvious because the plants are grown as terrestrial orchids. It would be possible that frequently potting materials are blamed for poor growth when other parts of the environment are really at fault.

The roots of Slippers, which occasionally grow as epiphytes and in some species always as epiphytes, carry a minute mycorrhizal fungus which lives in symbiosis with the plants, one assisting the other. This fungus is possibly essential to the germination and growth of paphiopedilum seed and equally many other orchid seeds. If root loss occurs any new root growth may need to pick up this mycorrhizal fungus to bring the plants back to full healthy growth. The other environmental necessities must also be present. It is a combination which is easily disturbed or destroyed. Too frequent use of fungicides, particularly the systemic or absorbed type, could cause failure of plants.

In embarking on Slipper cultivation as a specialist section of the pastime a grower should seek out all the information available, particularly for the individual species. In most instances the roots of hybrid paphiopedilums bear little resemblance to those of their progenitors. No single publication can give all the information and experience, committed to a notebook or memory, is a most reliable guide. Whatever information is available should be bought, copied or memorised. Not all of it will be true and not all will be of use if it is based on one particular cultivation region of the world or one sector of the orchid-growing community. *The two constant relevant factors are the creation of suitable artificial environments for the genus and an understanding of what the root systems should be doing.*

These features are applicable to any genera which are cultivated. The grower who sets out to specialise in a mixed species orchid collection has a great amount of work to do before becoming successful in it.

As we have begun by using Slippers as an example it is best to continue with them, because their root systems in cultivation are wholly terrestrial.

At the time of writing there were some sixty to seventy correctly named species and a number of species pretenders which should have been classed as simple varieties of well-known members. The root systems could be denoted as short or long and as moderately smooth, or hirsute—rough skinned. Each type has naturally developed to suit a different environment, and in cultivation will be modified to cope with development in containers.

Some of these root systems, such as that of *Paphiopedilum charlesworthii* (Rolfe), have developed to suit a calcareous or lime-based rock habitat. They are smooth or occasionally rough and capable of attachment to rock surfaces; they may develop length-wise for some distance in the search for food. In container culture this lengthening may be unnecessary, because the food source should surround the roots. But the inherent trait of the species is still present and the root systems should curl about the interiors of containers, and adhere to them if the surface characteristics are suitable. Such roots will produce good growth of glossy, well-reticulated dark green foliage, which should presage sturdy stems and finely coloured flowers with good substance. In a few words, the aim of the Slipper specialist.

The opposite type of plant would indicate that the system was totally wrong and should be recast. The specialist or would-be specialist should not need to be told of this, and would react instinctively to the bad appearance of the foliage.

A different type of root system is that of the Slippers with tesselated foliage like *P. bellatulum* (Reichenbach f.), although it is not a consistent feature of the whole group. The roots on cultivated plants are usually short and smooth, and are easily broken away from the bases of the plants because they are brittle. In the habitat they develop for easy attachment to rock surfaces and penetration of crevices in search of food. They are also freely produced from rhizomes.

In natural habitats these roots may grow quite long, but the length is usually lost when the plants are stripped away. This root type is difficult to redevelop in cultivation because it is impaired by use of containers. It is in some degree the type of root associated with such genera as sarcochilus. They are partly lithophytic.

In cultivation this failure to redevelop the root systems natural to plants has been the principal reason why so many Slipper fanciers have found the tesselated section of the genus such a miserable feature of their pastime, particularly if they sought to grow only one or two of the plants in an otherwise well-grown mixed orchid collection. Since the introduction of air flow systems instead of relying on natural ventilation their culture has taken a decided turn for the better and it is in this direction that the Slipper grower must turn his or her attention.

Continuity of growth, however, is still something of a problem and the Slipper specialist must take individual plant cultivation to great lengths to produce optimum results from a collection of species. There is a difference for some plants between the front of a bench or staging and the back. Few specimens will do well when buried in the centre of a mass of pots and foliage. Such changes in position may have as much effect as the upward or downward movement in developing adequate root systems. No fast results should be expected.

The third general type of Slipper root system is exemplified by *Paphiopedilum insigne* (Wallich) or *P. villosum* (Lindley). Both are part or almost total epiphytes with rampant root systems which are not stultified by containers. As epiphytes, these plants in their natural habitat are subject to periodic watering and dehydration, with all that it means and they are less fussy than the Slippers with tesselated foliage. The two groups are quite different types, with different needs, and should be separated in growing enclosures.

The roots of *P. insigne* and *P. villosum* are rough-looking and mostly covered with what looks like a dense mat of fine hair. They are particularly well illustrated in *Growing Orchids, Book One: Cymbidiums and Slippers*. This root type is easily damaged by poor culture or unacceptable growing material but perhaps is more tolerant than the shorter smooth group. The plants themselves have a more definite and lengthening rhizome structure than the tesselated group as a whole and this length gives a few more latent eyes for restructuring damaged root systems. In healthy plants the root system adheres tenaciously to the interior of containers, as one would expect of epiphytic plants. Although the epidermis or outer skin may be damaged in removal, the plant easily repairs and heals the tears or disregards them, and the root is capable of branching and resuming tip growth in good conditions. Not all the roots may be hirsute, but it is a characteristic of the type.

The principal feature of all paphiopedilum roots is that they have developed over their evolutionary period to sustain plants which have no moisture reserve capacity like those orchids which have developed pseudo-bulbs. They should not be severely dehydrated at any time, but their resilience is shown by the occasional appearance of flowers, sometimes well produced, on plants which have literally no live root at all. But this is not a habit, nor is it an advisable state in which a plant should flower.

If this kind of dehydration occurs in the natural habitat of Slipper species the plants die or become severely affected, and in glasshouse cultivation it may finally have the same result. It qualifies the recommendation that the genus as a whole, in species or hybrid form, should not be grown as an adjunct to a collection of epiphytes or form a minor part of any orchid collection. It could succeed, but with the best interests of the genus in the forefront it

Paphiopedilum root systems should resemble this example. It is proliferating in a friable, open potting mix with good moisture retaining composition. It is a good plan to occasionally up-end a pot in this fashion to understand thoroughly what is going on in the containers.

is inadvisable. An environment must be created for paphiopedilums which is suited to other similar genera not tied to such a seasonal life as epiphytic orchids.

All orchid plants lacking the moisture reserve capacity of pseudo-bulbs fall into the same cultural group as paphiopedilums, and should have root systems developed for constant or near constant moistness. Provided they come into the same cultural table of temperatures—and there is some flexibility here—they would be compatible genera to diversify most Slipper collections. It is not a prerequisite, as it is for paphiopedilums, that such orchids should be pot grown. They could be selected from a number of genera and noted as compatible because they are grown in baskets or suspended containers.

There is no reason why paphiopedilums should not be grown in sub-tropical and tropical regions, although it may be hard to pinpoint the area where cultivation fails. If it is the root system—and this is the most likely place—more attention should be given to the micro-climate in which the plants are placed. They will do best on a lower level, possibly on the floor of the growing enclosure and preferably with the containers bedded in moist material such as sand or a mixture of sand and coarse material like gravel, which will need to be contained and kept constantly moist to wet. This utilises the principle of cooling by evaporation. Provided the species have been well chosen and the foliage is adequately shaded there is no reason at all why specialist paphiopedilum collections would be impossible in some of the warmer areas in which orchids are grown. In the final analysis the root systems will dictate the health of Slipper plants and their ultimate flowering. If the nature and habits of the root systems are thoroughly understood, some of the recommendations of the previous paragraphs will be appreciated, based on the fact that the genus is grown as a terrestrial group.

All the other genera which are grown as terrestrial orchids— that is, with enclosed root systems—could in the first place be tried with the system outlined for paphiopedilums. The only factors which could go against them would be unsuitable environment or unsuitable potting material.

EPIPHYTIC ROOTS

The roots of natural growing epiphytic orchids proliferate in a 'soup' compounded of minute mosses, ferns, fungi and decaying organic material which is infected with a mycorrhizal fungus similar to that which assists paphiopedilum seed to germinate and grow.

The root systems are principally open and visible, although at times are entirely invisible and growing in a mass of detritus at the base of the plants. The Australian *Dendrobium falcorostrum* (Fitzgerald) is one of these orchids.

Although some, such as the Australian *Dendrobium speciosum* (J. E. Smith), also grow on rock surfaces and are termed lithophytes, they still come under the general heading of epiphytes.

It is probable that there was an even balance in numbers between terrestrial and epiphytic orchids before so much of both was destroyed by men and grazing animals. But in present reckoning it would appear that epiphytic orchids are disappearing more rapidly than their terrestrial counterparts.

The epiphytic orchids have a common feature. They have developed root systems which anchor the plants firmly as well as seeking out food. One could well ask how they locate food sources, and the simple answer would be that they lengthen and branch until a source is located. But after living with and growing these plants in the open and in enclosures, it seems to me that there is much more to it than that; one is induced to imagine that these roots have some sense of direction and are able to locate food sources at a distance from the body of the plant, and that in many instances *their host trees appear to make direct contribution to their nutriment.*

Each genus and each species is not necessarily conformist in this regard and we return to the proposition that each plant must find food or perish. An examination of the illustration of *Dendrobium speciosum* (J. E. Smith) on page 100, of *Growing Orchids, Book Four*, shows how long plants will continue the struggle to stay alive even though they cannot find enough food to enable them to produce flowers and ultimate seed.

A classic example of epiphytic support and feeder system roots is the cattleya plant, particularly if grown naturally. Few of us are concerned with the appearance or function of root systems in natural plant habitats, but an illustration indicating such a root system appears on page 62 of *Growing Orchids, Book Two*. It shows the considerable lacework of roots attached firmly to the bark of a live tree, penetrating every crevice in the bark if it is rough and corky and attaching to the very inner layers of the bark almost to the cambium layer itself. The roots growing from the rhizome, a section quite apart from the pseudo-bulbs, immovably prop, support and anchor such plants, however large they may become.

Because we grow most of these plants in containers we should give them rather large pieces of bark or other rough material in which to grow. This material could be rocky, but its purpose is to support the plants and anchor them through the penetrating root systems until such time as they are to be moved for further propagation as they outgrow containers. This move destroys much of the root system.

The conversion or subversion of these roots has been toward a system which entails neither anchorage nor searching for food, but a habit persists for wandering and becoming partly aerial.

It would be a mistaken view to imagine that things never go wrong in nature. They do go wrong, and drastically so at times. But as we are in control of nature in artificial cultivation it should not be so.

Cattleya roots are typical of many other epiphytic genera, varying from medium coarse to medium fine. There are exceptions in the genera, however, which could neither grow nor thrive in containers. A good example would be members of the rodriguezia group or another more exaggerated sequence in the Australian terete dendrobium catalogue.

Oncidiums comprise another group of these epiphytes with non-controllable root systems. As a whole they are a major genus of Central to South America, with medium-coarse to fine roots. The species grow in various climates and in general are not the best subjects for container cultivation. However, some members of the genus conform.

Plant size in the genus is no indicator of root size or a guide to the extent of its proliferation. They have evolved in climates from wet or dry tropical, wet and cold to temperate and mild, and it could be inferred from some that there is a relationship between root development and the climate in which they grow.

It is not possible to lay down rules, however, for any of them and two examples could be quoted which are both cool-growing yet have almost opposite types of root systems. *Oncidium excavatum* (Lindley) develops pseudo-bulbs much larger than those of *O. crispum* (Loddiges), yet it has fine proliferating roots while *O. crispum* has rather coarse cattleya type roots which will grow on slabs or penetrate into potting material.

Anyone wishing to specialise in the genus oncidium would need to create the three zones of warm, intermediate and cool to accommodate all the different representatives. This may be done to a degree by using the micro-climatic zones which exist in most enclosures. The system was written up in the *Australian Orchid Review*, Autumn Edition, 1985. A safe alternative would be to go through the complete list of the genus and select those which could be expected to conform. It should be mentioned, however, that their cultivation in specialist collections may be better suited to a warm natural climate and not recommended for any region where short summers with unreliable average temperatures are likely.

The oncidium section classed as equitant is very different from its generic associates. It is more likely to relate in cultural conditions to a tough, warm-growing group which includes plants like *Oncidium papilio* (Lindley), and the large-leafed group including *Oncidium luridum* (Lindley), which are native to the warmer and dryer regions of Central America and adjacent islands.

Most of these orchids should be grown with open root systems and given some scope to enter containers if they show inclination to do so. The system involves using sticks of treefern, bark or wood to which the plants are attached. The illustrations convey something which could be used as a pattern for this type of culture.

There are many thousands of epiphytes from which to choose, but they should be sorted into possibilities and not selected indiscriminately because they happen to come from a particular country. Natural wood containers such as slat baskets, sections of hollow branches and any natural container offer a better start for such epiphytic plants than plastic or terracotta pots. Some of the possibilities were illustrated in *Growing Orchids, Book Three*.

At times I have come under criticism for designating oncidiums as a dry-growing series and advocating aridity for some part of the annual cycle. The reality, of course, is that this was aimed at glasshouse cultivation, where for many months of the year the natural humidity is sufficient for many of the species. I do not have a choice in this regard because I consider the genus in total and not individually species by species. There is no doubt whatever that some of the species are not watered for months at a time or the result is inevitable root loss. But one would expect a specialist to take a collection plant by plant and note their requirements. *Watering plants means what it indicates—the plants are soaked. But that is quite different from the occasional swish with a hose.*

Dendrobium is a very numerous genus and the species embraced in it vary from those which grow in cold climates to those thriving in hot and brightly dry or hot and periodically wet areas. Australian examples are easy to nominate. For the hot and brightly dry region for most of its annual cycle a choice subject could be *Dendrobium dicuphum* (Mueller), from the Northern Territory; for the cold climate *Dendrobium falcorostrum* (Fitzgerald); and for the hot and periodically wet *Dendrobium bigibbum* (Lindley).

These dendrobiums are all what are known as hard-cane type and must be distinguished from the soft-cane group perhaps typified best by *Dendrobium nobile* (Lindley). If a distinction could be made it should be along the lines that in general the hard-caned dendrobiums should be grown with opportunity for open roots, while those of the soft-cane group are mostly subject to container cultivation. This rule is not inflexible, but is enough of a guide until each species is sorted into its category in any collection of the genus which may be established.

It is difficult to arrange a warm dry climate for some weeks or months in an enclosure. A compromise has to be struck and a system of culture worked out which will not kill the plants concerned but still has some semblance of the climate of the habitat. It becomes very difficult and must be considered a question of arranging a specialist collection and not expecting too much when growing such plants in mixed collections.

In the specialist collection we can select a dendrobium species and propose an environment to suit it. *Dendrobium bigibbum* (Lindley) could be quoted as an example. It is a subject more particularly for a warm climate where its growing season could commence at the right time—say, the beginning of October. This period of growth ends in early March, so the climate should be consistently warm and wet for the whole of it. By that time the flower spikes are well in evidence and grow without remission until the buds start to open in about two to three weeks. It can be seen by those requirements there is little chance of promoting such a program in a cold or irregular climate.

The program does not end there, because the plant in consideration must go into dormancy and remain almost dry until root and plant growth start again in October. In the meantime the conditions should be warm and slightly humid. It is obvious that an open root system of culture is needed, almost a clay pot minus potting material system which can absorb moisture and hold a root system in dormancy. In addition, such a proposition may suit few other dendrobiums—a compromise has to be worked out in the growing method, as suggested. The alternative in plastic pots would be for adoption of a rocky core material like scoria, which is used extensively in Queensland, or smooth river stones of a fairly coarse grade as in the illustration. In both instances the general idea is to give the root systems the utmost aeration and dehydration while still allowing ambient air moisture to sustain the plants. It is similar in many respects to cultivation of oncidiums.

Of course, it is easy to lay down the conditions which will suit one particular species. The difficulty is to arrange conditions in which some hundreds of the same genera will grow and thrive. All it takes is a little common sense and rejection of specimens which do not fit completely into the pattern. Among the collections which could successfully carry such orchids as *Dendrobium bigibbum* (Lindley) may be vandas or the warm-growing oncidiums. After all, this dendrobium can be grown in open garden conditions as far south from its habitat in Northern Queensland as Brisbane.

It could be said with truth that establishing an open-rooted epiphytic and specialist collection of orchids of any sort would need prior experience with orchids as a whole. The project is not one which could be taken on by a beginner without an unacceptable casualty rate. It would also need an appreciation of the importance of the relative climate of the place where it is to be established and then a most thoughtful selection of a main genus and its accompaniments.

The planning for accommodation is also a factor and some of the illustrations convey ideas for suspending plants, benching them and generally suiting them with environments which take note of the fact that their root systems are not only meant to be aerial but are also encouraged to adopt the mode.

OPEN ROOTS

Finally we come to totally aerial root systems. The term aerial could be misleading, because in cultivating some members of this section, such as vandas, epidendrums and other monopodial orchids,

The nature of root systems of various genera should dictate the type of culture, including potting material, size of containers and the frequency of watering. Two so-called terrestrial orchids, a cymbidium and a lycaste, illustrate the differences which should be noted.

The cymbidium (top) is growing in a sawdust-based compost (described chapter 3) while the lycaste, with its fine roots, has been grown in a common bark-based cymbidium mix. The cymbidium shows typical blackening of one root where the culture has been at fault and probably resulted in waterlogged compost. This is not drastic, as the other roots are quite clean and capable of further proliferation. They should be trimmed to get rid of any dead sections, and any instruments used flame sterilised.

The lycaste (bottom) exhibits typical structure of their normal root system, which is fine and profuse. If examined closely it will be found to have a furry exterior coat or epidermis. The root system is intact and the plant has obviously been well grown. Removed from a 12-centimetre pot (about 5 inches), it will be potted into a larger size.

The difference between the two potting mixes and handling the plants is that the cymbidium must be completely stripped of the old material and planted in fresh compost. This is obviously impossible or nearly so with the lycaste, which must be carefully transferred to a larger container without breaking up the root ball. The roots are clean, and the material is loose and friable and not decayed too far. The base of the larger container must be carefully crocked so that a new drainage area is formed below the root ball, which would quickly rot if allowed to become soggy. Also there should be no air pockets left in the container.

Open-rooted or totally epiphytic orchids offer cultivation problems when they must be suspended or mounted on objects to which it is hoped the roots will cling. The two illustrated are direct opposites, one being fine, short and dense, the other long, thick and dense. They have different origins and it is from these that a plan of cultivation should be worked out.

The thick-rooted orchids in the upper illustration are vandas, which produce roots from the main stem. They are known as monopodial and new growths seldom branch out from the main stem in cultivation. The plants were originally put into a slightly raised garden bed formed against a low cinder brick wall. Because of its porosity the wall attracted the vanda roots which became firmly attached to it, but a certain amount of root would grow into the garden bed if solid fertilisers were used as a top-dressing. The leaves have been cast from the main vanda stems from ageing and perhaps lapses in culture. If the wall is sprayed with fertiliser and water the roots will continue to branch and proliferate on it.

The other orchid is a dendrobium which grows naturally as a lithophyte on vertical or near vertical surfaces. The stems, for want of a better term, continually lengthen and produce short roots which attach the plant to a surface near enough for them to reach. This plant must be attached, preferably over its total pendant length, to some type of mount such as a long tree branch so that it can be cultivated as nearly as practicable in a natural manner. The section illustrated here was part of a plant more than a metre long. It would obviously be hard to fertilise a plant such as this unless the root system could attach to a surface.

a certain proportion of the roots become terrestrial if the food sources below the plants are attractive.

It has been my experience to find orchid plants which were totally aerial, hanging by only a thread or two of epiphytic root to a great length, developing a mass of aerial roots about the plants some metres below which were apparently capable of supporting and feeding them. I have also found vandas which were epiphytic, with no aerial roots other than one or two short protrusions from the main stem. Again I have found vandaceous orchids growing as masses on rocks on the ground, also with aerial roots, a number of which reached downward to find moisture and food. The term aerial must be qualified when used to denote genera with such habits, but in cultivation their systems are treated alike.

There are also differences within a genus such as vandas. Two types which may be quoted are those of the vandas with narrow or terete leaves such as *V. teres* (Roxburgh), which have thin, wiry roots that will cling to anything available, assisting the plant to climb until it can reach the best light source. Its counterpart, the broad-leafed vanda, has thicker roots which attach the plant to the surface on which the seed has germinated and grown. An example of the type is *Vanda tricolor* (Lindley), which has coarse rounded roots which flatten as they attach to surfaces, or which remain completely aerial, branching and proliferating to create networks about the plants.

Reed-stemmed epidendrums such as *E. ibaguense* (Humboldt, Bonpland and Kunth), with the occasional synonym *E. radicans* (Pavon), from the Central and South American region, a monopodial of similar morphology to vandas, create the same networks of roots which will remain aerial or travel down to enter food sources as necessary. Much of this root system is aerial and rather short when produced on the middle to upper extremities of the growths.

Monopodial genera such as renanthera, from tropical regions to the north and north-east of Australia, are aerial rooted, but they also produce anchoring root systems attached to hosts. *Plectorrhiza tridentata* (Lindley) is an Australian example, with its predominantly aerial root system produced to the extent which earned it the colloquial name Tangle Orchid. It is a beautifully scented species. Many orchids of the angraecum type are also aerial rooted to a degree, although some roots will enter potting mediums and containers.

The predominant feature of these orchids is their ability to absorb atmospheric moisture through open root systems as well as through foliage. The root systems are frequently rampant in cultivation. Some of the orchids come from hot, periodically humid climates which are principally dry, an example being the angraecums and associates. The parts of Africa and adjacent islands where they grow have climates of this nature for most of the year.

In *Southern African Epiphytic Orchids*, by John S. Ball, photographs of habitats illustrate what is obviously a hot and dry regime for most of the year. His description of the habitats of aerangis leaves no doubt of this. Other orchids accompanying the aerangis are acampe, angraecopsis, ansellias and similar hard-growing species.

It is obvious in considering plants of this nature that they need treating as individual specimens in collections. Few if any are capable of easy accommodation in containers mixed in with other orchids. Those which are so grown would naturally proliferate root systems outside the containers and probably commit the nuisance common to their kind by invading every other container within reach.

The proposition is that all these plants are self-selective and indicate the style of cultivation applicable to each. In general they are non-conformist compared with plants to which general principles may be applied, such as cattleyas and similar epiphytic orchids.

In most instances these plants must be suspended in containers with little or no potting material. These containers will retain them in token form and the plants and containers may be sprayed with weak fertiliser. This applies particularly to plants grown in sub-tropical and tropical regions, where humidity may be high for almost half the year. In cooler climates less suited to growing vandaceous orchids in quantity it may be necessary to devote a large area of glasshouse to hanging plants. This alters the whole design characteristics of growing areas.

There is no doubt that each species should be considered in its own right, and often great differences occur within a genus. For example, let us look at the Australian bulbophyllums and in particular two of them: *Bulbophyllum macphersonii* (Rupp) has small, tightly packed pseudo-bulbs growing on a slim rhizome from which issue fine, short roots; but *Bulbophyllum johnsonii* (Hunt and Rupp) has widely spaced pseudo-bulbs on a moderately robust rhizome considering the size of the plant, from which issues a fine but longer root system than the first named. Both these orchids are subjects for open-root culture and unsuitable for container cultivation. Such differences can be found in almost every genus. Perhaps it is possible to accommodate and train some of them into the form of culture we wish them to adopt, but in general a study of the plant in the first instance, an understanding of the root system and what it wants to do, and provision of the best possible means to encourage both will lead to successful cultivation.

Most of the illustrations in the other books and also in this volume are designed to assist in that understanding.

This survey of root systems has considered those of the principal cultivated genera in orchid collections. There are, naturally, large numbers of individual orchids for which cultural systems must be worked out. An example, perhaps extreme, is pleione. The genus in principle sacrifices the root system annually, together with the pseudo-bulbs, in a regular fashion which is understandable and for which cultural systems may be worked out by individual growers. Some believe in annual repotting; others leave the discarded root systems undisturbed in the potting material and wait for a second year's growth and flower before disturbing them.

Consider also the calanthes, which grow new pseudo-bulbs, perhaps rightly termed bulbs in this instance, each year; the old ones die and with them the root systems created to produce the flowers. The species which follow this pattern must at some stage produce two new bulbs from the one to be discarded in order that the genus will survive.

The orchid world is full of what humanity sometimes regards as peculiar plants and flowers. But nothing in nature is peculiar; it has been created, by whatever means, to take advantage of the situation it occupies. That we destroy them is not unusual, because man does not have a substantial background in anything very much—he is a destroyer.

EPILOGUE

The philosophical consideration of orchid growing does not answer very many of the questions about their culture, such as why do so many different people put in so much effort to confine plants to such unnatural processes. That is a big question and so many different answers could be put forward.

Why do they change their names so often? Is it a search for fame attainable in no other way, such as appears to drive some botanists and taxonomists forward? Is it a sense of trying to right a wrong which appears to have been done so many years before to a forgotten associate? Or is it simply a mundane commercial proposition generated by a demand? All these questions and more could be asked to account for the madness of the years of exploitation which caused the denudation of large areas of once beautiful forest of some of the components which made up the ecosystem.

By far the easiest proposition to interpret is the commercial one. But why did it become so big? This is in part understandable when the relative affluence of the community in general is considered compared with that of the early and middle years of the orchid history.

The magnitude is appreciated only by looking at the volumes of *Sander's List of Orchid Hybrids*. But this offers only a tiny segment of the total production line, which has turned again to duplicate the work of early hybridists lost along the way in the second century of the pastime.

The cultivation of species orchids also returned, but this time to a decimated natural source which, despite legislation aimed at protecting the remnant, is again being plundered under a system which sought to prevent it. As stated in another part of these books about growing orchids, this so-called protection opens the way for the exploitation of our natural resources in a way which is far worse than if it were left to the people themselves. If anything it is full of all sorts of loopholes through which the plunder continues. At times it is referred to as 'harvesting' our natural resources and it is not confined only to the plants in which we are all interested.

It is impossible to ask all these questions without a certain amount of self-examination. It could be asked with justification and propriety why the author began to grow orchids. The simple truth is that it was a part of childhood associated with plants and flowers which matured to an adulthood that could not leave that past experience behind.

But is that a good enough answer?

The beginning of the pastime so far as the author was concerned was along the usual lines—the purchase of plants from an existing grower and the addition of others bought wherever available—and it must be admitted that many of these were originally plundered from the natural resources of Australia.

It is very difficult to guess at the increase in the number of people growing the plants in the second century of their culture. But an educated guess could put it at a doubling and then again doubling and finally again doubling that figure by the 1980s decade. Any competent mathematician could work that out in percentage and the result of course would include all those people who have plants which they try to grow in all sorts of conditions. Orchids have become commonplace and included in the stock of that other bicentenary institution, the supermarket. The distribution system has become more simplified.

And what of the people who grow the plants because of a genuine love for them, just as the rose specialist does, or the dahlia specialist, or the gladiolus specialist such as the author's father? (He was also a field naturalist and at the age of three the author first learned about the orchids which grew adjacent to their home in what is now an inner suburb of Melbourne. They were 'Green-hoods'.) Perhaps the greater number comprise this last category.

But that still does not answer the questions. Possibly the only approach is for each grower to ask those questions of themselves and if nothing else it may help them to understand what 'makes them tick'.

BIBLIOGRAPHY

The following books from the private library of the author were used as reference material in writing the five books of the series:

PERIODICALS

Australian Orchid Review, 1936–86.
Orchadian (journal of the Australian Native Orchid Society), 1963–85.
Orchid Review, 1893–1986.
Orchid World, vols 1–6, 1910–16 (publication discontinued).

BOOKS

Anderson, Frank J., *Illustrated Treasury of Orchids* (reproductions of old lithographs), 1979.
Associacao Orquidofila de Sao Paulo, *Native Orchids of Brazil*, 1977.
Australian Native Orchid Society, *Checklist of Australian Native Orchid Hybrids*, 1981.
Australian Orchid Foundation, *The Orchidaceae of German New Guinea* (translated from German), 1982.
Ball, John S., *Southern African Epiphytic Orchids*, 1978.
Bateman, James, *The Orchidaceae of Mexico and Guatemala*, 1837.
Bedford, R., *A Guide to Australian Native Orchids*, 1969.
Braem, Guido J., *The Brazilian Bifoliate Cattleyas.*
Castle, Lewis, *Orchids, Their Structure, History and Culture*, 1887.
Chow Cheng, *Formosan Orchids*, 1970.
Clements, M., *Preliminary Checklist of Australian Orchidaceae*, National Botanic Gardens, Canberra, 1982.
Colombia: A Reference Guide, issued by 7th World Orchid Conference.
Cooper, Dorothy, *New Zealand Native Orchids*, 1981.
[de Oca, Rafael Montes?], *Humming Birds and Orchids* (illustrated by de Oca; translated by N. P. Wright), 1963.
Dockrill, A., *Australian Indigenous Orchids*, 1969.
Dressler and Pollard, *The Genus Encyclia in Mexico*, 1970.
Du Petit-Thouars, Aubert-Aubert, *Histoire Particulaire des Plantes Orchidées*, 1822.

Dunsterville, G. C. K., and Garay, L. A., *Venezuelan Orchids*, 6 vols, 1959–76.

Encyclopaedia Britannica, 1980.

Fitzgerald, R. D., *Australian Orchids*, 2 vols, 1977 (reprint).

Fowlie, J. A., *The Brazilian Bifoliate Cattleyas*, 1977.

Grant, Bartle, *The Orchids of Burma*, 1895.

Halle, Nicolas, *Flor de la Nouvelle Caledonie et Dependences, 8: Orchidees*, 1977.

Hawkes, Alex, *Encyclopaedia of Cultivated Orchids*, 1965.

Hoehne, F. C., *Flora Brasilica, Vol. 12, Orchidaceas, Parts 1 to 4.*

Japan Orchid Growers' Association, *Quality Stream 'Cattleyas'. The 800 Collection*.

Johns, John, and Molloy, Brian, *Native Orchids of New Zealand*, 1983.

Johnson's Botanical Dictionary, 1917.

Kupper, Walter, and Linsenmaier, Walter, *Orchids* (translated by Jean W. Little), 1961.

Laseron, Charles, *The Face of Australia* (first and revised editions), 1927–1949.

Lavarack, P. D., and Gray, B., *Tropical Orchids of Australia*, 1985.

Lecoufle, Marcel, and Rose, Henri, *Orchids*, 1957.

Lindley, John, *Sertum Orchidaceum*, 1838.

Morris, Brian, *Epiphytic Orchids of Malawi*, 1970.

Nicholls, W. H., *Orchids of Australia*, 1969.

Ortiz, Pedro, and others, *Orchideas Ornamentales de Colombia*, 1980.

Pabst, G. F. J., and Dungs, F., *Orchidaceae Brasilienses*, 2 vols, 1975–7.

Paxton's Botanical Dictionary, 1868.

Pears' Cyclopaedia, 1900, 1930.

Pocock, Maynard R., *Ground Orchids of Australia*, 1972.

Pradhan, Udai C., *Indian Orchids, Guides 1 and 2*, 1976, 1978.

Quisumbing, Dr Eduardo, *Philippine Orchids*, 1981.

Rentoul, J. N., *Growing Orchids, Book One: Cymbidiums and Slippers*, 1980.

———, *Growing Orchids, Book Two: The Cattleyas and other Epiphytes*, 1982.

———, *Growing Orchids, Book Three: Vandas, Dendrobiums and Others*, 1982.

———, *Growing Orchids, Book Four: The Australasian Families*, 1985.

Rolfe, R. A., and Hurst, C. C. H., *The Orchid Stud Book*, 1909.

Sagarik, Rapee, *Beautiful Thai Orchids*, 1975.

Sander, Frederick, *Reichenbachia*, 4 vols, 1888.

Sander's List of Orchid Hybrids, 6 vols, 1945–80.

Sander's Orchid Guide, Sanders (St Albans, UK) Ltd, 1927.

Saunders, W. Wilson (ed.), *Refugium Botanicum* (1869–1872–1882), 1980 reprint.

Schelpe, E., *An Introduction to South African Orchids*, 1966.

Schultes, R. E., and Pease, A. S., *Generic Names of Orchids*, 1963.

Schweinfurth, Charles, *Peruvian Orchids*, 4 vols and Supplement, 1958–70.

Stewart, J., and Hennessy, E. F., *Orchids of Africa*, 1981.

Stewart, Joyce, and others, *Wild Orchids of Southern Africa*, 1982.

Valmayor, Helen, *Orchidiana Philippiniana*, 2 vols, 1985.

van der Pijl, L., and Dodson, C. H., *Orchid Flowers, Their Pollination and Evolution*, 1966.

Veitch, James, *A Manual of Orchidaceous Plants*, 2 vols, 1887–9 (original edn).

von Drateln, Hermann, *Odontoglossum Culture*, [1960?].

Warner, R., and Williams, B. S., *The Orchid Album*, vols 2, 3, 4, 1883–5.

Waters, V. H., and Waters, C. C., *Survey of the Slipper Orchids*, 1973.

Williams, Brian, and others, *Orchids for Everyone*, 1980.

The proceedings of various Orchid Conferences were also referred to for useful information and data, as well as various publications of Alfred Russell Wallace.

Reference maps used were: *South America*, Kummerley and Frey; *Indonesia, the Philippines, Malaysia, Vietnam and other Asian countries* by Robinson; *Bangladesh, Sri Lanka, India, including Burma* by Bartholomew. Outdated references to boundaries and state changes were traced through the older encyclopaedias.

In consulting these and other references many conflicting facts were noted, and many mistakes were found, including some in what are usually considered impeccable sources. These were accepted as part of the processes of recording, interpretation and not least the printing and reproduction, and not held too unkindly against the authors.

Cross references from *The Orchid Review*, edited by Robert Allen Rolfe and others into the *Gardeners' Chronicle* were made available through the courtesy of the Melbourne Herbarium.

INDEX

Figures in italic indicate illustrations, either black and white or colour.